MW00659090

GOD'S LOVE IN THREE-PART HARMONY

Walking with the Lord is a journey that lasts a lifetime. If you enjoyed the *Opening Your Heart Series*, look out for these new Bible studies that will continue to nurture your soul.

THE KEEPING IN BALANCE SERIES

Harmony – Part I
How to find the balance between mediocrity and perfectionism and become the woman God created you to be without stressing.

Perspective – Part II
Become more content and grow stronger in the face of failure, and keep moving when you're tempted to settle for the status quo.

Exhale – Part III
Ideas for establishing a rhythm of rest, worship, and surrender and reorder your thoughts to create inner peace.

COMING SOON

THE DISCOVERING OUR DIGNITY SERIES

Tapestry – Part I
From relationship challenges, to the death of dreams, and the lure of compromise– how to apply age-old wisdom from the women of Genesis to the challenges of today.

Legacy – Part II
Explore a myriad of women's issues such as shame, loneliness, and making a difference in the world, and learn from the wisdom of ancient women.

Heritage – Part III
Inspiration about work and worship from key women in the New Testament, including Mary, the Blessed Mother, and her insights on what it means to live sacrificially.

For more spiritual inspiration or to learn more about Walking With Purpose, visit us at walkingwithpurpose.com

walking with purpose

You're also invited to join our community on Facebook, Twitter, Pinterest and Instagram.

walking with purpose

Dear friend,

Welcome to *Harmony*, part I of the *Keeping in Balance* young adult Bible study series! You have so many choices in terms of where you spend your time. Your generation is jam packed with ability, passion, and a desire to see change happen in the broken places of our world. I want to commend you for slowing down to tend to your interior places– the unseen parts of you that determine your character and sense of worth. So much calls out for your attention, but something within you is drawing you to a deeper place of reflection. That's the work of the Holy Spirit as He woos you to the heart of the Father. It's truly a privilege to be with you on this journey.

There is no question that your ideas and initiative can bring healing and light to places where woundedness and darkness run rampant. But if you don't take time to tend to all that lies below the surface in your heart, you won't make it to the finish line. Life is a marathon, not a sprint, and in the words of author and speaker Christine Caine, "If your gift and talent take you to a place where your character can't keep you, the gift that is on you will destroy you." Those powerful words make me pause and reflect on the importance of cultivating the soul, and I'm preaching to myself even as I share them with you.

I pray that as you endeavor to live a life of balance, these lessons would prove useful. They highlight areas that have been pitfalls for me, so I share these truths as a fellow learner more than an expert.

It's been said that this is the most visually stimulated generation in history. May we take our eyes off our screens and fix them on Jesus.

Running beside you,
Lisa Brenninkmeyer
Founder and Chief Purpose Officer of Walking with Purpose

Harmony

Keeping in Balance Series

Part I

www.walkingwithpurpose.com

Authored by Lisa Brenninkmeyer
Cover and page design by True Cotton
Production management by Christine Welsko

IMPRIMATUR + William E. Lori, S.T.D., Archbishop of Baltimore

The recommended Bible translations for use in Blaze and Walking with Purpose studies are: The New American Bible, which is the translation used in the United States for the readings at Mass; The Revised Standard Version, Catholic Edition; and The Jerusalem Bible.

Any internet addresses (websites, blogs, etc.) in this book are offered as a resource and may change in the future. Please refer to www.walkingwithpurpose.com as the central location for corresponding materials and references.

Printed: November 2018

ISBN: 978-1-943173-22-8

Keeping in Balance Series, Part I

TABLE OF CONTENTS

INTRODUCTION

LESSONS

APPENDICES

NOTES

Welcome to Walking with Purpose

You have many choices when it comes to how you spend your time—thank you for choosing Walking with Purpose. Studying God's Word with an open and receptive heart will bring spiritual growth and enrichment to all aspects of your life, making every moment that you've invested well worth it.

Each one of us comes to this material from our own unique vantage point. You are welcome as you are. No previous experience is necessary. Some of you will find that the questions in this study cause you to think about concepts that are new to you. Others might find much is a review. God meets each one of us where we are, and He is always faithful, taking us to a deeper, better place spiritually, regardless of where we begin.

The Structure of *Keeping in Balance* Series

The *Keeping in Balance* series is a three-part Bible study, each of which can stand alone, or all three can be completed one after the other. Each Bible study integrates Scripture with the teachings of the Roman Catholic Church to point us to principles that help us manage life's pace and pressure while living with calm and steadiness.

This Bible study can be used on your own, giving you great material for daily Scripture meditation and prayer. It also lends itself well to group discussion. We encourage you to gather your tribe—a handful of friends who want more out of their spiritual lives. The accountability and deeper friendship that will result make it so much easier to live out the truths contained in these pages.

Study Guide Format and Reference Materials

The three parts of *Harmony - Keeping in Balance Part I* are divided into three sections:

The first section comprises five lessons, which are divided into five "days" to help you form a habit of reading and reflecting on God's Word regularly. If you are a young woman who has only bits and pieces of time throughout your day to accomplish tasks, you will find this breakdown of the lessons especially helpful. Each day focuses on Scripture readings and related teaching passages, and ends with a Quiet Your Heart reflection, which should lead you to a time of personal prayer. In addition, Day Five includes a Saint's Story; a lesson conclusion; a resolution section, in which you set a goal for yourself based on a theme of the lesson; and short clips from the *Catechism of the Catholic Church*, which are referenced throughout the lesson to complement the Scripture study.

The second section, the appendices, contains supplemental materials referred to during the study.

The third section contains the answer key. You will benefit so much more from the Bible study if you work through the questions on your own, searching your heart, as this is your very personal journey of faith. The answer key is meant to enhance small group discussion and provide personal guidance or insight when needed.

A memory verse has been chosen for each part of the *Keeping in Balance* series, and we encourage you to memorize it as you move through the Bible study. An illustration of the verse can be found in the Introduction section, and a color version and phone lock screen can be downloaded from our website.

At the end of the book are pages on which to write weekly prayer intentions.

Walking with Purpose™ Young Adult Bible Studies

The *Opening Your Heart* Series

Beloved: *Opening Your Heart, Part I* is a six-lesson Bible study that lays a strong foundation for our true identity as beloved daughters of God. We'll learn that we belong to a family that will never abandon us. We'll encounter grace and practical tools to make God our first priority. Jesus will meet us personally in the pages of His Word, and we'll be transformed as a result.

Unshaken: *Opening Your Heart, Part II* is a six-lesson Bible study that fills our spiritual toolbox with exactly what we need to grow stronger in our faith. We'll discuss why and how we should read the Bible, what difference the sacraments really make in our lives, how to bravely face challenges in our efforts to follow Christ, and the way Mary perfectly mothers us through it all.

Steadfast: *Opening Your Heart, Part III,* a six-lesson Bible study, unpacks why we are hustling for our worth and how to conquer our fears. We'll look at the role of suffering and forgiveness in our lives, and dig deeper into how we can truly change in the areas where we have felt enslaved. We'll explore life purpose, our vocations, and the depth of God's personal love for His beloved children.

The *Keeping in Balance* Series

Harmony: *Keeping in Balance, Part I* is a five-lesson Bible study that helps us to get a grip on our lives by looking at the importance of authenticity, setting priorities, managing expectations, and having healthy relationships. We'll also explore finding a balance between mediocrity and perfectionism so that we can become the women God created us to be without stressing or striving.

Perspective: *Keeping in Balance, Part II* is a five-lesson Bible study that addresses how we can become more content, grow stronger in areas where we've failed a million times, and get moving when we feel like settling for the status quo. *Perspective* also explores how we can engage our culture as Catholics at a time when the reputation of Christians is at an all-time low.

Exhale: *Keeping in Balance, Part III* is a six-lesson Bible study that helps us establish a rhythm of rest, worship, and surrender. If you long for more simplicity in your life and are ready to order your thoughts so you can experience inner peace, this Bible study will both inspire you and provide you with practical steps to make positive changes.

The *Discovering Our Dignity* Series: *Coming Soon*

Tapestry: *Discovering Our Dignity, Part I* is a six-lesson Bible study that explores the beginning of salvation history through the eyes of the women of Genesis. The difficulties they struggled with are remarkably similar to our own: relationship challenges, the death of dreams, the lure of compromise, and the danger of self-reliance. We'll learn from their mistakes as we apply age-old wisdom to our modern challenges.

Legacy: *Discovering Our Dignity, Part II* is a nine-lesson Bible study that picks up where *Tapestry* left off. Our exploration of the women of salvation history continues as we move further into the Old Testament. We'll explore a myriad of women's issues such as loneliness, shame, leadership challenges, and making a difference in the world.

Heritage: *Discovering Our Dignity, Part III* is a seven-lesson Bible Study that highlights key women of the New Testament. Mary and Martha will help us explore the balance of work and worship, and the poor widow will shed new light on what it means to live sacrifically. We'll be inspired especially by Mary, the Blessed Mother, as we apply her wisdom to our daily challenges.

[1] Full-Color Free Printables available at walkingwithpurpose.com/free-printables.

Walking with Purpose™ Website

Please visit our website at www.walkingwithpurpose.com to find supplemental materials that complement our Bible studies; a link to our online store for additional Bible studies, DVDs, books, and more; and the following free content:

WWP Scripture Printables of our exclusively designed verse cards that complement all Bible studies. Available in various sizes, lock screens for phones, and a format that allows you to e-mail them to friends.

WWP Bible Study Playlists of Lisa's favorite music to accompany each Bible study.

WWP Videos of all Connect Coffee Talks by Lisa Brenninkmeyer.

WWP Blog by Lisa Brenninkmeyer, a safe place where you are welcome, where the mask can drop and you can be real. Subscribe for updates.

WWP Leadership Development Program
We are here to help you take your leadership to the next level! Through our training, you'll discover insights that help you achieve your leadership potential. You'll be empowered to step out of your comfort zone and experience the rush of serving God with passion and purpose. We want you to know that you are not alone; we offer you encouragement and the tools you need to reach out to a world that desperately needs to experience the love of God.

Links to WWP Social Media

Twitter, Pinterest, Facebook, Instagram

Lessons

NOTES

Lesson 1

BALANCE THROUGH AUTHENTICITY

Introduction

There's nothing like a job interview to tempt you to throw authenticity to the curb. When asked about your greatest area of weakness, who seriously dishes up the major flaws? Who talks about jealousy toward the friend who has everything you don't, your hidden addiction, or FOMO that makes eventually quitting any job a serious possibility?

Instead, we try to think of something that sounds humble and honest, but hopefully won't disqualify us– non-essential skills that we doubt have anything to do with the job description. We might mention that we aren't good at group presentations when we know the job won't require that. Or we say, "I triple-check everything on a spreadsheet and attend to details obsessively. Some would call that being a perfectionist– that's my flaw. But you can count on me to get the job done!"

It's exhausting to go from one interview to the next, desperate to be chosen. But it's even harder when we experience this dynamic in our relationships. We want to be accepted, wanted, desired, and included. We wonder what it takes to be enough. Figuring that filtered is better than flawed, we attempt to project an image of "perfect" when what we really feel is that we can't keep up.

How often do we say we're fine when we're not? There's a cost to this "image is everything" way of living. Our relationships remain superficial. The result? Loneliness. We may be surrounded by people, but we don't feel that they really know us. And we fear that if they did, they'd walk away. So we hide behind a fake exterior that we're trying really, really hard to keep polished and pulled together.

Living authentically means we drop the mask and embrace vulnerability. We stop acting like we're something that we're not. And for most of us, that is a terrifying thought. The minute we contemplate being real to this degree, fear kicks in. We fear we'll be rejected; that friends will be disgusted; that love will be pulled back. We worry that if we're really known in this way, if we're seen for who we truly are, we won't be worthy of connection. We'll be lonely. And although living behind a mask is its own version of loneliness, it seems safer.

So we try to live up to the expectations around us. We do our best to do it all, to do it perfectly, and for it all to appear effortless. We paste smiles on our faces and say we're fine, when we're anything but.

But what are we missing when we fail to live authentically? In all this effort to become who we "should" be, are we kept from becoming the amazing women we were created to be? Is our real life passing us by?

Day One
WHERE DID THIS HIDING BEGIN?

1. Adam and Eve have always been depicted without clothing in the Garden of Eden. Their nakedness is a picture of total vulnerability. It was safe to be naked in the garden because something was absent. This "something" is very present in our world, and blocks our ability to be authentic and vulnerable with one another. According to Genesis 2:25, what was absent from the garden?

Shame is not the same as guilt. When you feel guilt, you feel badly about something you have done. When you feel shame, you feel badly about who you are. It's the difference between feeling you *made* a mistake and feeling you *are* a mistake. Shame corrodes your ability to be authentic, because you're afraid to reveal your true self.

2. When God settled Adam in the Garden of Eden, He told him, "You are free to eat from any of the trees of the garden except the tree of knowledge of good and evil. From that tree you shall not eat; when you eat from it you shall die." (Genesis 2:16–17) Carefully read Genesis 3:1–5. How did the snake (the devil) get Eve to doubt God's goodness and disobey Him?

3. When did the hiding begin? What was the root cause of the perceived need to hide? See Genesis 3:6–10.

This is the first time we see a woman not wanting to be seen. Her fig leaves and the coverage of the trees were her attempt to avoid facing what she had done. But God loved her too much to leave her there. He called her out of the shadows and dialogued with her about her choice.

4. Read Genesis 3:13–23. As God discussed Adam and Eve's choice to disobey, He described sin's consequences. One of those consequences was separation from God; they would no longer be able to walk with Him in the garden. But God's desire was (and is) restoration and reconciliation. What evidence is seen in God's words to the snake in Genesis 3:15 that He had a plan to bring people back to Him, into an authentic, close relationship? Note: Read this verse and interpret "the woman" as Mary, the Blessed Mother, and "her offspring" as Jesus.

Genesis 3:15 gave hope that restoration was coming. While those in the Old Testament looked *forward* to the day their Redeemer would come, we look *back* to our Redeemer's victory on the cross. When Christ died on the cross and rose again from the dead, He destroyed "the works of the devil." (1 John 3:8) The devil wanted (and still wants) to keep people in darkness, certain that there's no hope for us when we sin. He wants to keep us in that place of shame that says, "You are a mistake, and there's nothing that can change that." But Jesus' death and Resurrection changed *everything*. He paid the price for our sin, so we don't have to. If we stop hiding from God and allow Him to truly see us, He will not reject us. If we ask, He will forgive us.

Quiet your heart and enjoy His presence. . . . Get real with God.

One place we can lack authenticity is in our relationship with God. We hide from Him, as if He can't see our sin. God invites us to see ourselves as He sees us. This is how we are described in 1 Peter 2:9–10:

> But you are "a chosen race, a royal priesthood, a holy nation, a people of his own, so that you may announce the praises" of him who called you out of darkness into his wonderful light. Once you were "no people" but now you are God's people; you "had not received mercy" but now you have received mercy.

He calls us out of darkness and into the light. He asks us to stop hiding our sins and instead lay them before Him in the light of His presence. This is authenticity with God. He has given us one of the sweetest promises ever in 1 John 1:9. He promises that if we'll stop hiding from Him, if we'll acknowledge our sins, He will be faithful and just and will forgive our sins and cleanse us of every wrongdoing.

Settle yourself in God's presence. Take off your mask. Stop acting as if He can't see into your heart. Stop believing the lie that if you tell Him your sins, He'll reject you. He will not. He will forgive you. Confess all that's on your heart. Connect to Him again. Enjoy what it feels like to be honest and authentic with God.

Day Two
WHAT KEEPS US STUCK IN SHAME?

Sin should draw us to confession, not to shame.

When we sin, the Holy Spirit begins to work in our souls (because that's where He is), and He *convicts* us. This is what we feel when we know we've done something wrong and we need to make it right. It's a call to confession.

By contrast, when we sin, the devil begins to work from outside us (because he is not within us), and he *condemns* us. He whispers shame in our ears (remember, outside in). The problem is, all too often we don't know how to differentiate between our own voices and thoughts, God's voice, and the devil's. So we listen to the voice that shames us, and we believe the lie that we aren't good enough, we never will be, that we *are* the sin. We're damaged, beyond repair.

But this is a lie, and believing it keeps us stuck in shame.

1. How is the devil described in John 8:44?

2. When people are trained to recognize counterfeit money, they do not spend their time studying the counterfeit. Instead, they make such a thorough study of the real thing that when they see something counterfeit, it immediately stands out as a fake. In that same way, the best strategy to help us recognize the devil's lies is not to focus on the way he's been messing with our minds for centuries. Instead, we should be saturating our minds with the truth of Scripture. What will be the result if we do this? See John 8:31–32.

3. How is Scripture described in Hebrews 4:12?

4. There is a battle that rages every day within your mind. The devil wants you to believe his lies, and God wants you to embrace His truth. How is this battle described in 2 Corinthians 10:3–5? What are we to do with every thought?

We get stuck in shame when we believe the devil's lies about who we are and who God is. This is why it is absolutely essential that we know Scripture. We need to go beyond just hearing it at Sunday Mass, to saturating ourselves with it *every day*. This is the best way for us to be able to discern whose voice we are hearing (the Holy Spirit convicting or the devil condemning). What we need to do is compare what we are hearing or thinking to what has been revealed to us in Scripture. What we read in Scripture is truth. If what we are hearing does not gel with what we have read in Scripture, then we know that what we are hearing is a lie. We hold the lie up to the truth, throw it away, and embrace what God says. That's taking every thought captive to Christ.

Quiet your heart and enjoy His presence. . . . Allow Him to renew your mind.

"Do not conform yourselves to this age but be transformed by the renewal of your mind, that you may discern what is the will of God, what is good and pleasing and perfect." (Romans 12:2)

Throw the garbage out and invite truth in to stay. Ask God to renew your mind—to replace your faulty way of seeing Him, yourself, and those around you with His truth. In what area of life are your thoughts condemning, negative, shame filled? Bring those thoughts into the light. Hold them up to the truth of God's Word. Throw out the thoughts that are not from God. Ask Him to replace them with His words of truth.

Day Three
WHERE SHOULD OUR SENSE OF WORTH COME FROM?

Vulnerability expert Dr. Brené Brown has done extensive research into shame. After thousands of interviews, she discovered a common denominator among people who are able to separate themselves from shame and live with authenticity and vulnerability. In each case, they have a deep sense of worth. They believe that they are worthy of being loved and of belonging. This gives them the courage to be seen for who they really are.

Our sense of worth is under constant attack. This is one of the key battlegrounds in our minds. We hear the following lies over and over again:

Your worth is measured by what you do.
Your worth is measured by whether or not you have a boyfriend.
Your worth is measured by how much you weigh.
Your worth is measured by what others think of you.

Lies are whispered into our minds, and it's our job to counter those lies with the truth of God's Word.

1. How can the truth in 2 Corinthians 12:9 help a woman who is struggling to believe that she is worth everything to God, even when she isn't accomplishing what she feels she should?

2. How can the truth contained in Romans 5:8 and Ephesians 2:4–9 help a woman to believe that she is worth everything to God, even when she is so aware of how far she falls short of His standard of holiness?

3. How can the truth contained in 1 Samuel 16:7 help a woman to believe that she is worth everything to God, even when she feels overweight and unattractive?

4. How can the truth contained in Psalm 139:1–16 help a woman to believe that she is worth everything to God, even if her own parents didn't love her or if people in her life today aren't caring for her as they should?

Quiet your heart and enjoy His presence. . . . Your life is hidden with Christ in God.

The truth is, our worth is not based on who we are. It is based on who God is. It is based on the one we belong to. We belong to God. We are His beloved daughters. The more we are able to focus on God and His worth, the more we can rest in His all-sufficiency. He is everything we need. We don't need to worry about anything being taken from us. We can lose our health, our money, our beauty, our achievements, our reputations, our relationships, but none of this will touch our worth. Your worth is not measured by any of those things. It has been measured in one place—the cross. At the cross, Jesus measured your worth and declared you worth everything. *He held nothing back. He gave His life so that you could live in freedom. And if the Son has set you free, you are free indeed (John 8:36)! Saturate yourself in this truth. Talk to the Lord about how worthy He is. Thank Him for counting you worthy of His love.*

Day Four
BEING AUTHENTIC WITH YOURSELF

Before we can explore being authentic in relationships, we need to check how authentic we are with ourselves. How often do we stuff our feelings in order to avoid conflict or to behave the way we believe a good Christian should? We can ignore our feelings to a point that we can't even recognize what's going on inside us. Peter Scazzero explores the detrimental effect of this in his book *Emotionally Healthy Spirituality*. He writes the following:

> To feel is to be human. To minimize or deny what we feel is a distortion of what it means to be image bearers of our personal God. To the degree that we are unable to express our emotions, we remain impaired in our ability to love God, others, and ourselves well. . . . When we deny our pain, losses, and feelings year after year, we become less and less human. We transform slowly into empty shells with smiley faces painted on them.[2]

1. How authentic are you with yourself in regard to the ways in which you have been hurt? Which of the following four descriptions do you most identify with? "I stuff my feelings." "I ignore my feelings." "I explode." "I share what I'm feeling in a healthy, balanced way." If you tend to stuff those feelings or ignore them, why do you think you do this?

[2] Peter Scazzero, *Emotionally Healthy Spirituality* (Nashville, TN: Integrity Publishing, 2006), 26, 70.

2. Do you remember how the snake spoke to Eve in the garden, insinuating that God was holding out on her? He does the same thing today. He tries to convince us that if we draw close to Christ, we're going to have to give up who we are and what brings us joy. What does Psalm 37:4 say about the desires of our hearts?

God didn't create us to be automatons—people without passions, dreams, and desires. In fact, God gives us healthy and wholesome desires because He wants us to experience joy. The devil tells us that following Christ is boring, and that we know best what will make us happy. God wants to explore our desires *with* us, to redeem the ones that He knows will ultimately not satisfy, and to help us achieve the ones that He knows will be good for us. He wants us to be the authentic women He created us to be, in touch with the desires of our hearts.

3. Women are natural nurturers and caregivers. It's easy for us to lose ourselves as we serve others. Do you feel selfish focusing on yourself? Do you know your authentic self well enough to express and embrace what truly brings you joy? If so, describe what fills you with delight and joy.

4. Many of us are afraid to dream. Fear of failure, lack of opportunities, jealousy over the abilities of others, and a steady reminder of our limitations can all get in the way. Take a moment to think about what you truly hope for. Let go of all the reasons why it can't be. List your dreams here.

Women often worry that thinking about what brings them joy, what they dream of, and what they hope for is self-centered behavior. But knowing who you are is simply being authentically *you*. That is healthy. What's unhealthy is making the achievement of these things your primary goal. Living selfishly occurs when you are determined to achieve these things at a cost to other people. Sometimes we'll have to say no to what we most desire, and although that is difficult, it's a part of surrendering our lives to

Christ. But when we don't even know what we hope for, we've lost touch with who we are. And that's not living authentically.

We will not achieve every one of our dreams and hopes. Not every moment in the day will be joy filled. But being aware of these desires in our hearts will help us to be on the lookout for the times when God delights us by bringing these things to pass. It'll help us to develop the virtue of gratitude. And we'll feel more fully alive as a result.

Peter Scazzero says it well:

> God plants desires in our hearts so we will nurture and water them. Often these desires and passions are invitations from God, gifts from him. Yet somehow we feel guilty unwrapping those presents. When I ask people, "Tell me about your wishes, hopes, and dreams," they are often speechless. "Why do you ask?" they respond. "Isn't my only wish, hope and dream supposed to be to serve Jesus?" Not exactly. God never asks us to annihilate the self. We are not to become "non-persons" when we become Christians. The very opposite is true. God intends our deeper, truer self, which he created, to blossom freely as we follow him.[3]

Quiet your heart and enjoy His presence. . . . He understands what you are feeling.

Jesus went before us and set us a wonderful example to follow in terms of living authentically. He was fully human, so He truly understands how hard it is to be us. He felt the same pressures that we do, yet He never lost Himself in His mission, or gave up and conformed to be who people wanted Him to be.

He started with the firm foundation of basing His worth and value on the right things. He didn't base it on people's opinions, His own accomplishments, or His possessions. He surrounded Himself with friends, and shared how He felt with them. When He needed help, He asked for it. He also practiced self-care. He didn't heal every person who was sick. When He needed to pull away to pray, He did. Everything about Him flowed from His union with His heavenly Father. He was authentically Himself, regardless of the pressures or circumstances.

So talk to Him about what you are feeling. He understands. He's listening. There's no need to edit your words or keep your emotions under control. Just let it all out.

---

[3] Ibid, 28.

Day Five
BEING AUTHENTIC WITH OTHERS

Once we've done the hard work of being authentic with God and with ourselves, we face the next challenge: being authentic with those around us. Whether or not we can do this will impact the quality of our close relationships, but that's not all that's on the line. Christians are increasingly being perceived as hypocritical, and as a result, many people who desperately need Christ are walking away. After the terrorist attacks of 9/11, church attendance swelled. Unfortunately, within a relatively short period of time, most of those people left. The Barna Group researched this and came to the following conclusion: September 11 gave churches an amazing opportunity to be a transforming presence in people's lives. But few people who showed up at church experienced anything that was sufficiently life changing to capture their attention. In essence, people came back to church and rediscovered why they hadn't been coming in the first place.[4] Would this have been different if they had seen Christ's followers living radically transformed lives? Might they have stayed if they saw a level of holiness, joy, and peace that had no explanation other than that God must be real and at work in lives today?

As Christ's representatives on earth, we have been asked to live our faith authentically. People don't want to *hear* what we believe (or read it in our status updates); they want to *see* what a difference Christ makes. Authenticity requires personal integrity. Having integrity has been described as doing the right thing, in the right way, for the right reason. Let's stand on the foundation of God's unconditional, personal love for us, and show Him our gratitude by living in this way.

1. What do the following verses have to say about how Christians should live? See Matthew 5:16, Ephesians 4:1–3, and 1 Peter 2:12, 15.

2. What we do matters. But how do we know the right thing to do? Where should we go for guidance? See Psalm 19:9 NAB, 119:105, and CCC 104 and 107.

---

[4] Barna Group, "How America's Faith Has Changed Since 9-11," November 26, 2001, https://www.barna.org/barna-update/article/5-barna-update/63-how-americas-faith-has-changed-since-9-11#.UwHv7_1S4c4.

3. Why we do what we do matters. What do the following verses teach us about the importance of our motives? See Matthew 6:1 and 1 Corinthians 10:31.

4. Does this mean that to be people of integrity we can never fail? No. The truth is, one of the best opportunities to be authentic and show personal integrity comes when we mess up. People can accept that Christians are imperfect. They'd just like us to be honest and humble instead of acting like we're something we're not. Jesus addresses this in Matthew 5:23–24. What does He say we should do before we come and worship Him? Is there a relationship in your life that God is asking you to tend to? Do you owe anyone a humble apology? What do you think would happen if everyone attending church on Sunday made the effort to seek reconciliation with his or her "brother" before showing up to Mass?

Quiet your heart and enjoy His presence. . . . Let Him infuse you with what you need to live authentically.

Dear God,

Help me to live courageously and authentically. Doing the right thing, in the right way, for the right reasons is hard. The truth is, I can cover up a lot of my sin with a well-constructed mask. But there's no freedom in living like that. Help me to remember that although it's painful to admit that I have been wrong, the alternative is to act like I'm someone I'm not. Help me to remember that when I admit I am flawed, my transparency allows others to admit their own struggles. It's the power of the "me too." Suddenly we don't feel so alone. We're able to grow in empathy. Thank you for becoming a man and sharing in the mess of humanity. Knowing that you understand the obstacles that I face helps me turn to you for strength and guidance.

Conclusion

An Australian nurse, Bronnie Ware, has spent years caring for patients in the final weeks of their lives. She was so struck by her observations that she wrote a book called *The Top Five Regrets of the Dying.* Common themes emerged that remind us of the importance of living authentically.

Here are the top five regrets of the dying, as witnessed by Ware:

1. I wish I'd had the courage to live a life true to myself, not the life others expected of me.
2. I wish I hadn't worked so hard.
3. I wish I'd had the courage to express my feelings.
4. I wish I had stayed in touch with my friends.
5. I wish that I had let myself be happier.[5]

Suppressed feelings had led to bitterness and often physical illness. The busyness of life had crowded out time with friends, and in the end, loneliness resulted. Many people had spent their lifetimes assuming that circumstances determined the course of their lives, not realizing that *choices* are what truly shaped them. Much of life had been spent pretending to be content, when dreams, desires, hopes, and preferences had never been truly owned and embraced.

If we want to live without regrets, it's clear that we need to embrace authenticity. It'll require leaving the comfort zone and dealing with some conflict. It means we don't settle for false peace, and instead do the hard work of reaching for the real thing. Is it easy? No. But the alternative, in the words of author and speaker Christine Caine, is becoming "actors in a drama rather than pilgrims on a journey." Let's not settle for that. Reach out and grab hold of your life—the messy, wonderful, imperfect, and authentic one you were created to live.

---

[5] Bronnie Ware, "Top Five Regrets of the Dying," Exposing the Truth, July 27, 2013, http://www.exposingthetruth.co/top-five-regrets-of-the-dying/#axzz2tEjmC2Sx.

My Resolution

"My Resolution" is your opportunity to write down one specific, personal application from this lesson. We can take in a lot of information from studying the Bible, but if we don't translate it into action, we have totally missed the point. In James 1:22, we're told that we shouldn't just hear the word of God, we are to "do what it says." So what qualities should be found in a good resolution? It should be **personal** (use the pronouns I, me, my, mine), it should be **possible** (don't choose something so far fetched that you'll just become discouraged), it should be **measurable** (a specific goal to achieve within a specific time period) and it should be **action-oriented** (not just a spiritual thought.)

Examples:

1. In order to live authentically before God, I'll go to confession. I won't hold back. I'll let Him into the dark places within me, and I'll ask Him to shine His healing light there.

2. Each morning, as a part of my prayer time, I'll allow myself to feel emotion before God. Then I'll journal any insights I receive.

3. There is something unresolved between me and another person. Instead of ignoring that, I will go to him or her to seek reconciliation. I will admit where I have been wrong, and will ask for forgiveness. I'll let go of the myths that I am always right, that I have to be perfect, or that vulnerability is a sign of weakness. The truth is, it takes courage and strength to be authentic.

My Resolution:

Catechism Clips

CCC 104 In Sacred Scripture, the Church constantly finds her nourishment and her strength, for she welcomes it not as a human word, "but as what it really is, the word of God." "In the sacred books, the Father who is in heaven comes lovingly to meet his children, and talks with them."

CCC 107 The inspired books teach the truth. "Since therefore all that the inspired authors or sacred writers affirm should be regarded as affirmed by the Holy Spirit, we must acknowledge that the books of Scripture firmly, faithfully, and without error teach that truth which God, for the sake of our salvation, wished to see confided to the Sacred Scriptures."

Verse Study

See Appendix 2 for instructions on how to complete a verse study.

2 Timothy 1:7

1. Verse:

2. Paraphrase:

3. Questions:

4. Cross-references:

5. Personal Application:

Lesson 2

BALANCE THROUGH PRIORITIES

Introduction

In the beginning there was perfect balance. There was enough time to do what was needed. The pace of life wasn't frenzied. Everything the eye could see was beautiful. Equality and peace characterized the male and female relationship. There was no hunger or weariness. Life was good.

This perfect balance created a world of freedom. There was no need to worry. Absolute trust in God's goodness took away all fear of the future. Only one thing was required of the people living in paradise: They were not to eat from one particular tree. That was it. Just one thing needed to be avoided. God knew that if they ate from that tree, they would think they knew everything and would forget to trust Him.

The comfort of a perfectly balanced life was enjoyed until a lie tipped the scales. A serpent persuaded a woman that she knew better than God. Believing the lie that God was holding out on her, she became convinced that she was missing out. She was the first to question God's unconditional love for her, but certainly not the last. The perfect balance was lost.

That balance had been held in place by man's right relationship with God. It wasn't just God's rule that had been broken. His heart broke, His relationship with His children was damaged, and the perfect world He'd created to delight them was now going to be full of things that didn't work. Life would feel messy, stressful, imbalanced.

But God loved too deeply to leave things un-mended. A Rescuer was promised and a journey began. Generation after generation waited. Long years passed. Then in an unexpected way, in the most unlikely of places, when very few realized it, *He came.* The Rescuer was born to a woman who succeeded where the first woman had failed. Although the rescue plan wasn't what she had expected, she *trusted.* She put God first. She made pleasing God her highest priority—above her reputation, her security, her plans. This supreme act of faith released the Lover of our souls into the mess of our existence. He came to help us find the way back to God, back to the life we were created for.

Is this the life you're longing for? You are invited on this journey. There's no better time to begin than today. Come as you are. Come with a desire to be transformed. Your Rescuer is waiting.

Day One
PUT GOD FIRST

If we want to live balanced lives, this is the starting point. Putting God first lays the foundation, and if we miss this or try to diminish its importance, our lives will become shaky very quickly.

1. Why should God be the highest priority in our lives? Read the following verses, noting specific reasons why God deserves to hold first place in our lives and hearts. It has everything to do with who He is and what He's done.

   Revelation 4:11

   John 3:16

2. In the Old Testament book of Exodus, we read the story of God rescuing His people from slavery in Egypt. When God led the Israelites out of slavery, He gave them rules that they would need to follow if they were going to fully experience freedom. They didn't know how to be free; all they had known was slavery. And what would be sadder than being free but still acting like a slave? To help His people walk in freedom, God said, "I am the LORD your God, who brought you

out of the land of Egypt, out of the house of slavery. You shall not have other gods beside me. You shall not make for yourself an idol." (Exodus 20:2–4) In other words, God was to be their first priority. This was the key to living in freedom.

We've been delivered from slavery, too. We weren't enslaved by Egyptians; we were slaves to sin. Our freedom wasn't earned. It was given to us as a gift, grace from a loving God. Because of the suffering and death of Jesus in our place, we are "no longer a slave but a child, and if a child then also an heir, through God." (Galatians 4:7)

We have been given freedom, but what do we risk if we do not make God the first priority in our lives? See Galatians 4:8–9 and 5:1.

3. Anything or anyone we place as a higher priority than God will create pressure He never intended. If we make financial stability or achievement the highest priority, we'll find that we never have enough. Even when we're experiencing success, fear of losing it all will nip at our heels. If we make a person our highest priority, the pressure put on that relationship will guarantee dissatisfaction and conflict. We cannot expect any person, no matter how wonderful, to be to us what only God has promised to be. Are you experiencing pressure that might be caused by making something other than God your highest priority?

Quiet your heart and enjoy His presence. . . . Come as you are.

"It is not that I have already taken hold of it or have already attained perfect maturity, but I continue my pursuit in hope that I may possess it, since I have indeed been taken possession of by Christ [Jesus]…forgetting what lies behind but straining forward to what lies ahead, I continue my pursuit toward the goal, the prize of God's upward calling, in Christ Jesus." (Philippians 3:12–14)

God knows that we aren't perfect. Don't be discouraged if upon reflection you see many things that you have prioritized above God. Forget what lies behind, and look forward to what lies ahead. God meets us where we are, and simply asks us to take the next step toward Him. Press on.

Day Two
PUT PEOPLE NEXT

Read Matthew 22:34–40.

Have you ever had any of these thoughts?
I'm overwhelmed!
Just look at all I have to get done!
It's all *important.*
What am I supposed to do, not sleep?

Jesus cuts through the chaos, giving us some basic principles that we can apply to our heaving to-do lists. Two things are crucial. We covered the first on Day One: giving God the place of highest priority. The second will be our focus today: After God, people come next.

1. What did Jesus say was the second-greatest commandment? See Matthew 22:39.

2. The principle of "loving your neighbor as yourself" works only if you treat yourself well. Do you habitually neglect yourself, forsaking prayer, rest, good nutrition, exercise, and healthy emotional boundaries? In which areas of your life would you like to love yourself better? Do you agree that this is a necessary first step in order to love others well?

3. List the most important "neighbors" that God has placed in your life. This list can certainly contain geographical neighbors, but it should also include family and friends. This is not a list of everyone you know. These are the key people whom you sense God would like you to pour your life into. Circle the priority relationships on the list. Do those priority people receive your best, or do they get your relational leftovers?

4. Reflect on an average day in your life. How much of your time is spent pouring into your most important relationships? Have tasks and to-dos begun to crowd out time for loved ones? If so, what is one change you could make this week to create time to love your neighbor? Remember, when Jesus talked about love in Matthew 22, *love* was used as a verb. We can feel love in our hearts but fail to show it in our actions. The love Jesus calls us to involves more than good intentions. It requires movement.

Quiet your heart and enjoy His presence. . . . He wants to love others through you.

How we approach our priorities has a lot to do with how we define success. If we consider success to be measured by what we accomplish, then we'll have a hard time putting people ahead of our tasks. It's important to remember how God measures success. At the end of our lives, God isn't going to ask about all that we have accomplished. He will look at how we've loved. This is the true measure of significance. Have we loved well? Sacrificially? With abandon?

Loving well requires time. It also requires that we depend on God. More often than not, the love required of us will exceed what we feel we have. This is why it's so essential that we put God first, starting our day in prayer. We come to Him in prayer, believing Jesus' words to us in John 15:5: "I am the vine, you are the branches. Whoever remains in me and I in him will bear much fruit, because without me you can do nothing." We attach ourselves to Him, and ask Him to fill us with His divine love. When the demands we feel are greater than our own resources, something beautiful happens. The divine love spills out, and it's like the fine wine that Jesus saved for last at the wedding at Cana. Instead of giving people our leftovers, we give them what is best—God's love—released because of our weakness and dependence on Him.

Day Three
MAKE TIME FOR YOUR GOD-GIVEN PASSION

"For we are his handiwork, created in Christ Jesus for the good works that God has prepared in advance, that we should live in them." (Ephesians 2:10)

You were created with a divine purpose. This means that there are good works that God prepared in advance specifically for you. God executes His plan for mankind through His children, and He equips and calls you to take part. Wise women take the time to identify their spiritual gifts, ask God to reveal specifically what He wants them to do, and then respond to His call.

Read 1 Corinthians 12:4–11.

1. A. Who has spiritual gifts? See 1 Corinthians 12:7.

   B. Where do the spiritual gifts come from? Who is the source? Do we get to choose which gifts we want? See 1 Corinthians 12:11.

We don't always recognize the gifts that He has placed within us. It's our responsibility to discover them.

2. List the spiritual gifts described in 1 Corinthians 12:8–10. Note that this is not an exhaustive list of the spiritual gifts.[6]

[6] Other lists are found in Ephesians 4:11, Romans 12:6–8, and 1 Corinthians 12:28–30.

3. What is the purpose of spiritual gifts? Are they to be used for personal gain or glory? See 1 Peter 4:10 and CCC 799.

Note: The Catherine of Siena Institute (www.siena.org) has wonderful resources to help you identify your spiritual gifts.

Quiet your heart and enjoy His presence. . . . He wants to fill you with Himself so you can be His hands and feet in the world.

When we take the time to discover the spiritual gifts that God has given us, we take an enormous step closer to discovering the specific call He has placed in our hearts. We come to a place where we humbly recognize our skills, and we see how those strengths can be used in an area that we feel passionate about. What do you see in the world that is so not right that you can barely stand it? Could it be that God is calling you to do something about it? Take a few moments to talk with Him about this.

Day Four
VALUE THE UNSEEN

A desire for instant gratification runs strong in the current of our culture. To deny what we want now for something better later goes against our natural instincts. But if we determine to prioritize what is most important, we'll look at our choices with a longer range perspective.

1. A. How does 2 Corinthians 4:17 describe our difficulties, and what does it claim they are producing for us?

B. Our difficulties don't feel "momentary" or "light", but God is inviting us to look beyond what they feel like to what they are doing for us. What does Romans 5:4 say that affliction does for us?

Obviously, this kind of transformation doesn't just automatically happen. It's what is possible when we walk through difficulties. But we always have a choice– to become bitter or better, resigned or resolute, discouraged or determined.

2. Where does 2 Corinthians 4:18 tell us to place our focus? Why?

"What is unseen is eternal." This is talking about a focus on heaven. It's a picture of living life with the end goal in mind.

3. The world we live in celebrates a life that looks good on Instagram. A life where suffering is present but being patiently borne, where character is being sought more than celebrity, that type of person tends to go unnoticed. And that's hard. We *all* want to be seen. According to Hebrews 12:1, who is watching us?

Who is in this "great crowd of witnesses"? To find the answer, we have to look at the preceding chapter in Hebrews. Hebrews 11 is called the Hall of Faith, because it talks about faithful men and women in the Old Testament who are now in heaven. The "great crowd of witnesses" includes them, but also the saints.

4. What are the saints in heaven watching us do? See Hebrews 12:1.

This race that we run is a marathon, not a sprint. To successfully run a marathon, you need endurance. The character quality of endurance doesn't come naturally to us. We don't want to have to wait for anything. If someone doesn't text us back IMMEDIATELY it feels like a catastrophe. Especially when we can see that the message was read. Endurance isn't something that we just "get", it's something that we need to build. As we saw in Romans 5:4, we get the opportunity to build it anytime our circumstances are different than what we want.

5. Hebrews 12:1 tells us that if we want to run the race that lies before us, we need to rid ourselves of every burden and sin that clings to us. What do you need to throw off in order to run your race well? Is it a relationship that is holding you back from being sold out for Christ? Is it an addiction? A coping mechanism that you go to instead of going to God? Is it people pleasing? Is it a constant checking of social media that is leaving you discontent instead of inspired? List it here.

   Who is someone you could ask to hold you accountable as you set out to throw off this burden or sin?

Quiet your heart and enjoy His presence. . . . invite the Holy Spirit to infuse you with faithfulness.

"I have competed well; I have finished the race; I have kept the faith. From now on the crown of righteousness awaits me, which the Lord, the just judge, will award to me on that day, and not only to me, but to all who have longed for his appearance." 2 Timothy 4:7-8

St. Paul wrote those words just before the end of his life. He, along with the host of heaven, is hanging over the rail, watching you and waiting to see what you will do with the baton of faith. Will you run your race? Will you keep your eyes fixed on Jesus (Heb. 12:2), or will you keep looking to the left and the right to see how other people are running their races?

This is your moment. Your one wild and beautiful life. Fix your eyes on Jesus who is standing at the finish line, waiting to welcome you and tell you what an amazing job you have done. Show up and press on through the hardships. Allow the pressure to refine you instead of fearing that it will destroy you. If you are waiting for the perfect time or for things to come together before you start to run, you're going to miss it. This *is your time.*

Day Five
JESUS, OUR EXAMPLE

Read Mark 1:35 and John 8:28–29.

1. Jesus offers us the supreme example to follow. What do Mark 1:35, John 8:28–29, and CCC 2602 reveal about the way in which Jesus prioritized?

2. Prayerfully list your top five priorities in order of importance.

    1.

    2.

    3.

    4.

    5.

3. Look at how you have spent time this week. Can you identify activities that have been time wasters? How could you use that time better to live according to your priorities?

4. If it were possible to start from scratch and clear your schedule, what large and small things would you make time for?

Quiet your heart and enjoy His presence. . . . Let Him guide your schedule.

God never intended for us to feel the pressure of "doing it all." He made us, and He knows our limits. Each day, He waits for us to turn to Him so He can reveal to us the things that are most important and those we can let go of. This is very hard for us to discern without the Holy Spirit's guidance. So much in life feels urgent. We fear the consequences of leaving things undone. God has the big picture, and longs to help us out of this place of pressure.

Come to God in the morning (or right now) with your calendar. Ask Him to reveal to you the things that are most important from His perspective. Ask for Him to help you to be sensitive to His still, small voice throughout the day so that you can see interruptions as divine appointments. At the end of the day, place all the things that didn't get done in His very capable hands. Trust Him with all that you cannot carry or solve.

"Teach us to count our days aright, that we may gain wisdom of heart." (Psalm 90:12)

Conclusion

It's so easy to fall into the trap of looking at everything at once, as if it all has equal importance and needs to be done immediately. All the events of the day will not be crowded into one hour. All the goals of a lifetime will not be achieved in a year.

One of the greatest mistakes we can make is to try to do in one season of life what God has meant for a later one. When we come at life full of enthusiasm, dreams, plans, and goals, it can be hard to say no to the good in order to say yes to the best. But that is exactly the self-discipline that we must have if we are going to be able to live out our priorities.

It's so much better if we can take each day as it comes, considering whatever is at hand to be God's will for that moment. You can receive your day from Him piece by piece. God will give you work to do. He recognizes that you need strength to carry out His plan. This is what He provides.

We are not left alone to figure this out for ourselves. Jesus prays for us without ceasing. Mary loves to intercede on our behalf. The Holy Spirit dwells within us, strengthening us to do what seems impossible. God pours love over us daily, constantly reminding us that our value doesn't depend on what we do or don't do. So press on to live life according to the right priorities, but never forget that you are covered by grace, and His grace is enough.

My Resolution

In what specific way will I apply what I learned in this lesson?

Examples:

1. I'll choose a "prayer spot" where I'll spend time with God daily. I'll put my Bible, rosary, Bible study book, prayer journal, and anything else that will help me pray in this one place. I'll put "time with God" on my calendar, and honor it as I would any other appointment.

2. I'll identify one time waster in my day, and replace it with an activity that has more value.

3. If I don't know my spiritual gifts, I will take a Spiritual Gifts Inventory in order to begin the journey of discovering my God-given passion.

My Resolution:

Catechism Clips

CCC 799 Whether extraordinary or simple and humble, charisms are graces of the Holy Spirit which directly or indirectly benefit the Church, ordered as they are to her building up, to the good of men, and to the needs of the world.

CCC 2602 Jesus often draws apart to pray in solitude, on a mountain, preferably at night. He includes all men in his prayer, for he has taken on humanity in his incarnation, and he offers them to the Father when he offers himself. Jesus, the Word who has become flesh, shares by his human prayer in all that "his brethren" experience; he sympathizes with their weaknesses in order to free them. It was for this that the Father sent him. His words and works are the visible manifestation of his prayer in secret.

Verse Study

See Appendix 2 for instructions on how to complete a verse study.

Isaiah 43:19

1. Verse:

2. Paraphrase:

3. Questions:

4. Cross-references:

5. Personal Application:

Lesson 3

BALANCING EXPECTATIONS

Introduction

Do you have a picture in your head about how life is supposed to be at your current age? Maybe you thought that by this point you'd be in a serious relationship, but you're worried that you're friendzoned for life. Have you projected forward, thinking about the perfect time to at a certain place in your career, or the best age to get married or start a family? If you're a dreamer or a planner, it's impossible not to have an opinion about how you'd like life to roll out.

We can be driven by expectations, and they come at us from many directions. We don't want to let anyone down, least of all ourselves. The more our expectations are met, the more powerful they can become. The fear of failure can increase with success. On the other hand, all too often our plans and timing do not match what God allows, which can breed disappointment and disillusionment.

So what should we do? Let go of hope? Lower all expectations and settle? Or hunker down and determine that if we believe in our dreams enough and work our tails off, somehow we can make it all happen?

I believe that we can find a balance in between those extremes. While it's true that unmet expectations can lead to heartache, God does promise us a future full of hope (Jer. 29:11). He is able to do abundantly more than all we can ask or imagine (Eph. 3:20).

Jesus came to earth and showed us an alternative way to live. He didn't stress out over disappointing people in His life or set expectations for Himself that were unrealistic and unhealthy. With His help, we can turn over a new leaf and experience peace, regardless of our circumstances.

Day One
OTHERS' EXPECTATIONS OF ME

1. Make a list of key people in your life and some things that they expect from you.

2. Do any of the people and expectations you listed make it difficult for you to make God the highest priority in your life? Did Jesus promise us that it would be easy to balance people's expectations with God's demand for first place in our lives? See Matthew 10:34–39, paying special attention to verse 39.

3. The following is a difficult truth to accept: *You will disappoint people.* It is utterly impossible to please all the people in your life. It's especially hard to face this fact when your sense of worth is tied to others' opinions of you. When you allow your worth to be measured by anyone other than God, you are in treacherous territory. Never forget, God has already determined your worth. When Jesus died on the cross for you, He emphatically declared, "You are worth *everything.*"

   In what practical ways can you fill up on God's love, so that your security is found more and more in Him?

Quiet your heart and enjoy His presence. . . . Let His love fill you so you don't go looking for it in the wrong places.

"But seek first the kingdom of God and his righteousness, and all these things will be given you besides." (Matthew 6:33)

When God asks us to make Him our highest priority, it's not because He's on an ego trip. God knows that we will only experience the deep fulfillment that we were created for when we seek it in Him. What a tragedy it would be if we found our earthly relationships satisfying enough that we never went searching for a relationship with our Creator. In order to draw our hearts to Him for all of eternity, God created us with a desire for happiness and peace that can only be found in Him. Even the most profound human relationships will always fall short of our deepest desires. People will disappoint us, and we will disappoint people. God created a place within each of us that is to be filled only by Him. Nothing else will satisfy.

Ask God to reveal to you the specific unhealthy expectations of others who are holding you back from the life He created you for. Which relationship needs to be brought to a healthier place? Ask God for the strength to set healthy boundaries. Ask Him for the grace to break the habit of people-pleasing. Go to Him for love, knowing that even if the people in your life are angry, He is enough.

Day Two
MY EXPECTATIONS OF MYSELF

1. Make a list of some of the things you expect from yourself. Thinking about your dreams and standards will help you identify them.

   Now go back and underline any expectations that are probably unrealistic during this season of your life.

   Then circle the expectations that you believe matter to God. To help you discern this, ask yourself, "If I don't meet this expectation, will Christ be upset?"

2. When you fail to meet the expectations you have for yourself, what thoughts go through your mind? How do you view yourself in those moments? What is your reaction when you disappoint yourself?

There are times when our expectations for ourselves are in areas that are not important to God. Failure in those areas gives us an opportunity to evaluate what matters most. Perhaps those expectations weren't worth pursuing in the first place.

Sometimes we have expectations in areas that God does care about. He wants us to grow in intimacy with Him and in holiness. It isn't wrong for us to have expectations and hopes in the area of spiritual growth. The problem isn't always the expectation itself. Often, it's how we react when we fail. Do we wallow in self-pity? Do we quit? Do we turn to escapism? God wants us to get back up and persevere on our journey of growth.

3. The way God responds to our failures is often different from the way we typically respond. How does God relate to us when we are weak and fall short of perfection?

   Matthew 9:10–13

   1 John 1:9

   Matthew 11:28–30

The word *yoke* (found in Matthew 11:29) comes from the Greek word *zugos. Zugos* can also be translated as "yoke," or "a balance, a pair of scales." It's as if Jesus was saying, "Take off your old yoke. It represents a way of weighing what's most important, and it's a broken scale. Replace it with my yoke. Replace it with my pair of scales. You'll find rest when you measure things as I do. What I consider most important each day isn't heavy. It isn't burdensome."

4. As you reflect on the expectations you listed in question 1, can you identify any that you are willing to let go in order to find rest? List them here.

Quiet your heart and enjoy His presence. . . . You will find rest for your soul.

It's very hard to let go of our expectations when we continue to measure our worth with a faulty scale. If our worth is tied to what we achieve, then the drive to be acceptable, good enough, or extraordinary will kick into gear, impacting our actions and attitudes. Good days will be ones when we meet all our expectations. They will be rare.

Grace-healed eyes look at life differently. They recognize that our worth was measured in one place, the cross. When Jesus died in our place, He declared us worth everything. Our worth isn't tied to what we do. It's tied to whose we are. We are God's beloved daughters. Toss out the old scales. They are only making you miserable.

Let grace do its healing work. Rest in the arms of your Father. Close your eyes, and just sit in His presence. Let Him love you. Be at peace.

Day Three
MY EXPECTATIONS OF GOD

1. What are your expectations of God? They have been shaped by your life experiences, your worldview, and things you've been taught about Him. Think of times you may have felt disappointed by or angry with God. This will help you identify your expectations of Him.

2. One of the reasons it's important to know Scripture is because it contains God's promises to us. Often, we expect things of God that He never promised. We can make the mistake of taking a Bible verse out of context, basing an expectation of

God on that verse, and later being disappointed when things don't go the way we expected them to. We need to know the whole truth. We need to know what God promised and what He *didn't* promise, and adjust our expectations accordingly. Read the following Bible verses, paraphrasing them in the space below.

Did God promise that Christians wouldn't suffer if they were faithful to Him? No.
But He did promise that . . .

Isaiah 43:2

Did God promise that if we are obedient to Him, he'll get rid of our weaknesses and make the road in front of us easy? No.
But He did promise that . . .

2 Corinthians 12:9–10

Did God promise that we'd always feel His presence? No.
But He did promise that . . .

Psalm 139:1–10

Did God promise that His children would be healed from illness if they prayed hard enough and had faith? No.

But He did promise that . . .

Psalm 23:4

In the face of our need, what God promises over and over again is Himself. He promises His presence. We cry out for relief, health, comfort, a miracle, and He promises: I am here for you. And I am enough. Regardless of our circumstances, regardless of what we feel, we can count on the promise that God "is not far from any one of us." (Acts 17:27)

3. According to CCC 397, what is the core issue when we question God's goodness in the face of unmet expectations?

Quiet your heart and enjoy His presence. . . . He is with you, always.

It's hard to trust God when you can't see or feel Him. Author Ravi Zacharias says it well:

> This longing to be touched is also the reason many Christians question God when they struggle to live life well and in a manner that brings glory to God, especially when they are going through a time of darkness or fear. We would love to feel God's arms around us. We would love to feel the embrace of the Almighty when we are feeling abandoned and alone. How many times have we wished we could just hear his voice? To the true seeker, sooner or later God comes through, even though his touch may not be recognized until much later. You see, instead of spectacular manifestations of power, the same God who used the human hand to write the Scriptures and preserve the written Word uses the human touch of his children to restore broken lives around them. This is the way Jesus conquers sin.[7]

God is not far off. He is here. His love never fails. That love is often delivered through the hands and hearts of His people. "Blessed be the God and Father of our Lord Jesus Christ, the Father of compassion and God of all encouragement, who encourages us in our every affliction, so that we may be able to encourage those who are in any affliction with the encouragement with which we ourselves are encouraged by God. For as Christ's sufferings overflow to us, so through Christ does our encouragement also overflow." (2 Corinthians 1:3–5)

Take some time to prayerfully reflect on the many times you have received God's love through the hands of a person. Thank Him for those gifts.

---

[7] Ravi Zacharias, *Has Christianity Failed You?* (Grand Rapids, MI: Zondervan, 2010), 87.

Day Four
HOW MY EXPECTATIONS AFFECT OTHERS

Many studies have been conducted to show the impact that expectations have on behavior. Whether the expectation is negative or positive, people tend to live up to what is expected of them. That being said, this portion of the lesson will not be focused on how our expectations of others can influence their behavior. Instead, we'll look at the ways in which people around us can be harmed by our reactions when our expectations go unmet.

Read Colossians 3:12–15.

1. What character qualities are we to display according to Colossians 3:12–15?

2. What things really derail you and cause you to come unglued? Which expectations trigger that reaction?

3. How do you typically react when those circumstances derail you? Be specific. Who is impacted by your reaction?

When you can see that an expectation is not going to be met, it's a red flag that you're about to be triggered into behavior that you're likely to regret later. It can be helpful to take a moment to ask yourself, "Who is going to be more affected (me or others) if this expectation is not met?" or "Will Christ be upset with me if this expectation is not met?"

4. Which quality described in Colossians 3:12–14 do you need most when unmet expectations knock you sideways?

5. Expectations can have such a hold on us that we often feel our reactions can't be helped. Some common responses to unmet expectations are listed below. Describe an alternative response based on the corresponding Scripture passage.

   "I'm just so disappointed. I can't help how I reacted."
   Joshua 24:15

   "I can't control my emotions."
   Philippians 4:13

   "I just can't take it anymore!"
   2 Corinthians 12:9

Quiet your heart and enjoy His presence. . . . Let the peace of Christ control your heart.

When your expectations are unmet, how does it impact the atmosphere where you live, study or work? Take some time to prayerfully meditate on the way in which your reaction to unmet expectations affects a specific loved one. Try to put yourself in the other person's shoes. How does it feel? What difference would it make in his or her life if you could let go of unrealistic expectations?

If you feel that your reaction to unmet expectations has not reflected the Christian character described in Colossians 3:12–15, could you ask forgiveness from God and from the person who has been hurt by your reaction? Could you take the next step and ask someone to hold you accountable to grow in this area?

Remember that God's mercies never fail. We can be changed, by the power of the Holy Spirit. We can break free from the chains of past responses. Freedom awaits.

Day Five
HOW JESUS DEALT WITH EXPECTATIONS

1. Just like us, Jesus dealt with family expectations. Describe what was expected of Him by His parents and how He responded to that expectation. See Luke 2:41–49.

2. What was the expectation of two of Jesus' closest friends? Did Jesus meet their expectation? See Mark 10:35–45.

3. Jesus also encountered expectations from the community. What did the people expect of Him in John 6:14–15? How did He respond to that expectation?

4. Had Jesus simply met the expectations of the people in each of the preceding examples, they would have missed out on something so much better. God's plan far surpassed their expectations. Did they realize this in their moment of disappointment? No. The superiority of God's plan wasn't revealed until later. How fortunate we are to have so many examples in Scripture that serve to remind us of the importance of patiently waiting for God. Can you think of an example from your life when God didn't act as you'd expected, but time later revealed that He was working out a far better plan?

Quiet your heart and enjoy His presence. . . . Patiently trust His timing and perfect plan.

"They that hope in the LORD will renew their strength, they will soar on eagles' wings; they will run and not grow weary, walk and not grow faint." (Isaiah 40:31)

Has your life turned out as you expected? Do you regularly experience disappointment when things don't go as you planned? Spend some time in prayer, asking God to give you patience to trust His timing and plans. Tell Him your hopes and dreams. Place them in His hands. Ask Him to guard them, and to bring them to pass if and only if they are what He knows to be best. Ask for the faith to accept His will, even if it's not what you expected.

Conclusion

Expectations are so powerful that we often become enslaved to them. We can feel as if we are suffocating under our own expectations and those of others. But we have a choice. We can let go of unhealthy expectations and choose to live freely according to what God desires and expects of us. That yoke is easy, and the burden is light.

What does God expect of us? This is summarized well in Micah 6:8: "You have been told, O mortal, what is good, and what the LORD requires of you; only to do justice and to love goodness, and to walk humbly with your God"

God doesn't expect perfection; He knows that we are human and prone to failure. Instead of perfection, He asks us to pursue holiness. And how does God measure holiness? By how we love. Primarily, He wants us to love Him. Then He wants to see that authentic love well up in our hearts and spill over into the lives of those He places in our paths.

God knows this isn't always easy. Truly selfless love comes at a cost. It can be painful. As Padre Pio said, "The life of a Christian is nothing but a perpetual struggle against self; there is no flowering of the soul to the beauty of its perfection except at the price of pain."

If we imagine the soul as a flower, many of us are tightly closed buds. There's great beauty within, but we haven't yet begun to open up to reveal all that's there. Our souls begin to bloom one petal at a time as expectations are surrendered to the Master Artist's hand. This growth is painful. We hold tightly to expectations because they are tied to our hopes, dreams, standards, and the way we believe life should be. It's hard to let go.

The only way we'll be willing to surrender our expectations is if our trust in God's love is greater than our desire to do things our own way. Our trust will grow in direct proportion to the amount of time we spend with God. A heightened awareness of Him causes us to see how He smooths the way for us each day. The alternative is to rush through our lives, focusing on the execution of our expectations. When we go at this pace, we're too busy to notice God's hand guiding, protecting, and blessing us. As a result, our trust in Him stagnates. We forget that He has the whole picture and the best plans. Our prayer time can quickly become the appointment when we give God His marching orders for the day. This is a sure recipe for disappointment.

Because of the indwelling Holy Spirit, no matter how much we may feel our expectations are hardwired within us, we can break old habits. We can see the flowering of our souls to the beauty of their perfection, one step at a time. As our souls burst into bloom, we'll be able to spread everywhere the sweet fragrance of Christ.

"But thanks be to God, who always leads us in triumph in Christ and manifests through us the odor of the knowledge of him in every place. For we are the aroma of Christ for God. . . ." (2 Corinthians 2:14–15)

My Resolution

In what specific way will I apply what I learned in this lesson?

Examples:

1. I'll go to adoration this week to sit in God's presence and soak up His love. Every time I'm tempted to please people in order to affirm my worth, I'll remember that nothing fills me or validates me like God's love.

2. I'll ask a friend to hold me accountable as I prayerfully endeavor to let go of a specific unhealthy expectation.

3. I will memorize one of the verses from Day Four, question 5. I'll ask the Holy Spirit to bring this verse to my mind whenever I am about to respond to an unmet expectation in an unhealthy way. This will help remind me that I always have a choice in terms of my response.

My Resolution:

Catechism Clips

CCC 397 Man, tempted by the devil, let his trust in his Creator die in his heart and, abusing his freedom, disobeyed God's command. This is what man's first sin consisted of. All subsequent sin would be disobedience toward God and lack of trust in his goodness.

Verse Study

See Appendix 2 for instructions on how to complete a verse study.

Isaiah 26:3

1. Verse:

2. Paraphrase:

3. Questions:

4. Cross-references:

5. Personal Application:

Lesson 4

BALANCE IN RELATIONSHIPS

Introduction

In 2012, the political newsmagazine *The Week* reported the following about a quarreling couple in Israel:

> A man from southern Israel has divorced his wife because she brought 550 cats into their home. The man, apparently not a cat lover, told the rabbinical court in Beersheba that he was unable to sleep in the bedroom because the surface of the marital bed was constantly covered in cats. He complained that the pets wouldn't let him get into the bathroom, got in the way of him preparing meals in the kitchen and also stole his food. The couple attempted reconciliation at the behest of the court, but the wife chose her cats over her husband.[8]

Can't you just hear the husband saying, "Can the record please show that *I* am not the problem?" And isn't this what you and I want the record to show anytime things get a little dicey in our relationships?

"I am not the problem. I'm not the one leaving the toilet seat up."
"I am not the problem. I pick up after myself."
"I am not the problem. When I finish the cereal, I throw away the box."
"I am not the problem. I'm not the one with the anger issue."
"I am not the problem. I'm not the one saying one thing to her face and another behind her back."

The care and keeping of relationships isn't easy. There are days when we all can relate to the bumper sticker that reads, "The more people I meet, the more I like my dog." People can be demanding and unbalanced, and we often wonder if we can count on their unconditional love. And frankly, people can be really annoying—especially when they don't do things the way we do, when our way is *clearly* the right way.

---

[8] "Best Articles: Britain," *The Week*, June 9, 2012.

As in all areas of our lives, God wants to step into the mess and make things better. This week, let's venture into the deep, into the heart of what matters. Let's take a look at balancing our relationships.

Day One
A GENUINE NEED

"I've been hurt. I need to protect myself. I don't want to need anyone." Once burned, many of us hesitate to open our hearts in relationships. Sometimes we need a reminder of why good relationships are worth the struggle to create them.

1. What do we learn from Genesis 2:18–25 and CCC 372 regarding God's perspective on the necessity of relationships?

We were created for community and were never meant to go it alone. God's plan has always been for us to experience authentic, vulnerable relationships with one another. Unfortunately, sin and selfishness entered the world, and as a result, many of our experiences have been fraught with hurt and disillusionment. The following questions and Bible verses will help us identify the qualities that should be found in our relationships.

2. Describe the benefit and necessity of having people who are willing to speak truth in our lives. Contrast this with what results when we surround ourselves with people who just tell us what we want to hear. See Proverbs 27:6 and 17 and Galatians 6:1.

We show wisdom in our relationships when we consider the spirit in which words are spoken and embrace any truth that's found in the hard-to-hear words of a friend.

Receive the words and examine your heart. Is there sin you need to confess? If so, what a gift those words are!

3. Sometimes we don't need to be told how we can improve; we just need to be loved and accepted as we are. What do Ecclesiastes 4:9–12 and Galatians 6:2 say about the role of encouragement in relationships? How can you encourage someone today who may be feeling lonely or discouraged?

4. Reflect on a relationship that has been painful for you. Look back at the qualities of good relationships that have been described in the preceding Bible verses. Are some of those qualities missing from that relationship? Is there someone you know who has those qualities that you would benefit from investing time in?

Quiet your heart and enjoy His presence. . . . You are never alone with God by your side.

Take some time to prayerfully reflect on the qualities that you look for in key relationships. The people closest to us will influence us the most. What do you look for in a friend? Have you valued things that are of little value to God? Have you sought accountability and authenticity? Have you made the effort to bear the burdens of others and encourage them? Ask the Holy Spirit to shed light on any changes that you need to make in terms of what you look for and pursue in relationships.

Day Two
CREATE BOUNDARIES

Is it OK for a Christian to set boundaries if it means that needs around her will go unmet? Absolutely. The key is recognizing when to say yes, and when to acknowledge limitations with a gracious but firm no. Healthy relationships require boundaries.

1. A. Read Galatians 6:2–5. According to verse 2, what are we to bear for one another? What are we to bear ourselves (verse 5)?

A *burden* is something oppressive or worrisome.[9] It's hard to bear a burden alone. By contrast, a *load* is an amount that can be carried at one time.[10] Loads are made up of the things we're all expected to do for ourselves. We are to help one another with burdens, but be responsible for our own loads. When do we get into trouble? When we find ourselves either carrying others' loads or refusing to compassionately help others carry their burdens.

B. Reflect on the difference between a burden and a load. Do you find yourself carrying others' loads or expecting them to carry yours? Do you help others with their burdens? Do you allow others the gift of helping you with your burdens?

2. According to Proverbs 22:3, "The astute see an evil and hide, while the naïve continue on and pay the penalty." Sometimes setting boundaries means creating emotional or physical distance. This is especially true when a relationship has been abusive. What should you see before you give trust again? Read the first part of Luke 3:8.

Genuine repentance will produce change. Words of repentance are a good first step, but they must be backed up with actions. You can forgive someone yet still need to maintain a safe emotional or physical distance from him or her.

---

[9] *Merriam-Webster Online*, s. v. "burden," http://www.merriam-webster.com/dictionary/burden.

[10] *Merriam-Webster Online*, s. v. "load," http://www.merriam-webster.com/dictionary/load?show=0&t=1385405406.

3. Many of us have been in a relationship with a controlling person. Establishing boundaries with such a person can feel scary. This is because neither option is very appealing—you either set the boundary and risk losing the relationship, or remain imprisoned to his or her demands. "God's plan is for us to be loved enough by him and others, to not feel isolated—even when we're alone."[11] We need to know in the depth of our being that *we are loved and not alone* in order to have the courage to set boundaries. Read the following verses, and describe God's personal love for you: Romans 8:35–39 and Ephesians 3:17–19.

4. We were created to love, and when we fail to love, we fail to measure up to our greatest potential (see John 13:35). Difficulties arise when we equate love with meeting every need we encounter. Even Jesus didn't meet every need or heal every disease, and He is God. We all have limits, and as a result, we need to discern what God is asking us to do, and what we are tempted to do out of guilt, fear, or other wrong motives. If we can't say no, there will come a point when we are unable to say yes to something God wants us to do. There are only so many hours in the day. What attitude does God want us to have when we help others? See 2 Corinthians 9:7. Are we being loving if we are motivated by fear? See 1 John 4:18.

Quiet your heart and enjoy His presence. . . . He is enough.

When we fill up on God's love, we are less apt to make decisions based on a fear of losing relationships or of making someone angry. God fills us up through the indwelling Holy Spirit, and "where the Spirit of the Lord is, there is freedom!"[12] *We're free to love. Boundaries give us the space to make decisions based on freedom and love.*

Dear Lord,

In which of my relationships do I lack healthy boundaries? Help me to discern which of my actions are motivated by fear and which are motivated by genuine love.

---

[11] Dr. Henry Cloud and Dr. John Townsend, *Boundaries: When to Say Yes, How to Say No to Take Control of Your Life* (Grand Rapids, MI: Zondervan, 1992), 67.

[12] 2 Corinthians 3:17

Day Three
CONFLICT RESOLUTION

1. How do you typically respond to conflict? Do you avoid it? Address it head-on? Stuff your feelings? Explode with emotion?

2. What should we do first when we encounter interpersonal conflict? See Matthew 18:15 and CCC 2478.

3. If the person in question doesn't respond to a direct, one-on-one conversation, what should the next step be? See Matthew 18:16.

4. When we engage in conflict, it matters *how* we say what we say. What insight do we gain into this from James 3:17?

In her book *Unglued*, Lysa TerKeurst explores how things fall apart when our reactions to our emotions aren't under God's control. Sometimes we explode with unrestrained emotion, and other times we stuff our emotions and ignore them. Neither is a good option. "In processing unglued reactions, soul integrity is the heart of what we're after. Soul integrity is honesty that's godly. It brings the passion of the exploder and the peacemaking of the stuffer under the authority of Jesus where honesty and godliness embrace and balance each other."[13]

Quiet your heart and enjoy His presence. . . . Reflect on Jesus' example.

Jesus was the perfect example of truth-telling under the control of the Holy Spirit. He didn't stuff His emotions or say He was "fine" when He wasn't. But when He spoke the truth, He did it without destroying the heart of the other person. His desire was always to see restoration. Spend some time prayerfully reflecting on the way you deal with conflict. Does your honesty need to be tempered by gentleness? Does your kindness need to be more honest? Ask God for help in your area of weakness.

Day Four
WATCH YOUR WORDS

1. If you could change the way you communicate in one relationship, which one would it be? What pattern would you like to see changed?

2. In the book of Ephesians, Saint Paul wrote about the quality of talk that should come out of the mouths of followers of Christ. List the qualities described in Ephesians 4:25–32.

3. When you come face-to-face with God's standards for your words, how does it make you feel? Discouraged? Motivated?

[13] Lysa TerKeurst, *Unglued: Making Wise Choices in the Midst of Raw Emotion* (Grand Rapids, MI: Zondervan, 2012), 52.

4. According to Luke 6:45, where do our words come from? If this is the place where our difficulty with words is rooted, do you think that simply improving our communication skills and techniques will solve the problem? What does God provide to help His children experience victory with their words? See Ezekiel 36:26.

Quiet your heart and enjoy His presence. . . . Be strengthened by His mercy.

Dear Lord,

I wish I could say that my words have always been truthful and life giving, but far too often, my words have been weapons that have caused harm. Please forgive me.

Use the following questions to aid your time of confession, and remember, "If we acknowledge our sins, he is faithful and just and will forgive our sins and cleanse us from every wrongdoing." (1 John 1:9)

Have my words stirred up dissension? (Proverbs 6:16–19)

Have I seduced with my words? (Proverbs 7:21)

Have I said too much and spoken in haste? (Proverbs 10:19, 29:20)

Have my words been reckless? (Proverbs 12:18)

Have I gossiped? (Proverbs 18:8)

Have my words been nagging? (Proverbs 21:9)

If we feel discouraged when we recognize how high God's standard is for us, we are in the perfect position to learn a very important lesson. In our own strength, we can't live the way God asks us to. It is only through Christ's strength that we can experience victory. We'll look at how this occurs on Day Five.

Day Five
OUR ONLY HOPE

Read Ephesians 1:15–23.

1. Saint Paul prayed that the eyes of our hearts would be enlightened so that we would know what important thing that belongs to the call of Christ? See Ephesians 1:18.

Hope. Biblical hope goes beyond desiring something that is out of reach. It is *expecting with confidence.* Where does this hope come from? It comes from "Christ Jesus, our hope." (1 Timothy 1:1) Because of Him, we can believe that our old patterns can change. This means that we can no longer say, "My communication with my husband is never going to change." In Jesus, there is hope for stale marriages. As mothers, we can't give in to discouragement and assume that the resistance our children have to our words will never soften. In Jesus, there is hope for children with attitudes and rebellion. What about the bitter or hurt friend? That isn't beyond Christ's redemptive power, either. In Jesus, there is hope for strained friendships.

2. According to Ephesians 1:18, what other benefit do we receive in our inheritance among the holy ones?

Riches. The riches that we receive from Christ give us everything we need in order to live life the way God desires. This is described in 2 Peter 1:3 in the following way: "His divine power has bestowed on us everything that makes for life and devotion." This means that when we are in the middle of a difficult conversation, *in that very moment,* God is supplying us with what we need to move beyond our hurt to speak words that build up and restore. We only need to draw from those riches. The alternative is to draw our words from our anger, pride, or desire to protect our ego.

3. What does God make available to those who believe, according to Ephesians 1:19?

When we say we can't speak the way that God desires, He replies, "I know you can't. That's why I inspired Saint James to write, 'No human being can tame the tongue. It is a restless evil, full of deadly poison.' (James 3:8) No *human being* can tame the tongue, but *I can.* I am inside you through the Holy Spirit. And that is the difference maker. My son, Jesus Christ, the Word,[14] will powerfully speak His words through you because He is in you. And that changes everything."

4. Read Ephesians 3:20, and put it in your own words. What difference does the truth of this passage make in terms of your communication challenges in your relationships?

Quiet your heart and enjoy His presence. . . . He dwells in your heart.

Take some time to meditate on the significance of the Holy Spirit dwelling within you. Do you draw on His strength and power, or are you more apt to try to solve your relationship problems independently? Talk to Him about the relationships you find most challenging. Ask Him to speak through you in each of those interactions. Do this today, and every time you enter into a difficult conversation. You don't need a lot of time to pray this prayer. As you find yourself in the minefield of a challenging conversation, silently pray, "God, speak through me! Give me your words to speak!"

[14] John 1:1

Conclusion

Author Gary Thomas shares the following insight into an alternative way to approach a common frustration in relationships:

> "instead of focusing your energy on resentment over how sparsely [someone] understands you, expend your efforts to understand him or her. As a spiritual exercise, find out what [his or her] day is really like. Ask her. Ask him. Draw them out—what is the most difficult part of your day? When do you feel like just giving up? Are parts of your day monotonous? Is there something you constantly fear? Take time to do an inventory of [their] difficulties rather than [their] shortcomings."[15]

It's all about perspective. The more we grow in empathy, the more we'll reflect Christ in our relationships. Who more than Jesus understands how difficult people can be? He was hassled, misunderstood, betrayed, battered physically and emotionally, and killed for something He didn't do. When we are frustrated in relationships, He gets it. But He never lets us off the hook in terms of how we should respond. He went before us, setting an example of speaking the truth in love, truly listening in order to understand what was in each person's heart, and engaging instead of getting offended. He didn't meet every temporary need He encountered, but He met the deepest need of every human heart. His love went the distance. He loved to the death, not because He was a doormat, but because His sacrifice meant that we would never have to be alone again.

He has not left us to manage our relationships alone. His very nature has been placed within us and is made effective in us, by the indwelling Holy Spirit. This is our hope. This is what keeps us from giving up. When we say, "I can't," the Holy Spirit asks that we trust Him to work through us. Nothing and no one is beyond the reach of God's hand. "May the Lord give might to his people; may the Lord bless his people with peace!" (Psalm 29:11)

[15] Gary Thomas, *Sacred Marriage: What If God Designed Marriage to Make Us Holy More Than to Make Us Happy?* (Grand Rapids, MI: Zondervan, 2000), 66.

My Resolution

In what specific way will I apply what I learned in this lesson?

Examples:

1. I've identified a relationship in which I need to establish some boundaries. I recognize that this isn't going to be easy to do, so I will find someone trustworthy to hold me accountable. I'll ask him or her to check with me on how consistently I am maintaining this new boundary, which will give him or her permission to speak the truth to me.

2. When conflict hits, I am more likely to talk about it to someone who isn't involved than to take the courageous action of speaking directly to the person who has hurt me. I will stop this pattern of gossip. Instead, I'll turn to God in prayer, asking Him if this conflict is something I can overlook. If I sense that it's something that truly needs to be addressed, I'll go directly to the person involved, as we're told to do in Matthew 18.

3. I will try to reflect Christ in my relationships not simply through self-effort. I recognize that if I'm relying only on myself, I will fail. Instead, I will start each day by asking the Holy Spirit to work through me, specifically in the area of a troubled relationship.

My Resolution:

Catechism Clips

CCC 372 Man and woman were made "for each other"—not that God left them half-made and incomplete: he created them to be a communion of persons, in which each can be "helpmate" to the other, for they are equal as persons ("bone of my bones . . .") and complementary as masculine and feminine. In marriage God unites them in such a way that, by forming "one flesh," they can transmit human life: "Be fruitful and multiply, and fill the earth." By transmitting human life to their descendants, man and woman as spouses and parents cooperate in a unique way in the Creator's work.

CCC 2478 To avoid rash judgment, everyone should be careful to interpret insofar as possible his neighbor's thoughts, words, and deeds in a favorable way:

> Every good Christian ought to be more ready to give a favorable interpretation to another's statement than to condemn it. But if he cannot do so, let him ask how the other understands it. And if the latter understands it badly, let the former correct him with love. If that does not suffice, let the Christian try all suitable ways to bring the other to a correct interpretation so that he may be saved.

Verse Study

See Appendix 2 for instructions on how to complete a verse study.

James 3:16

1. Verse:

2. Paraphrase:

3. Questions:

4. Cross-references:

5. Personal Application:

Lesson 5

BALANCE BETWEEN MEDIOCRITY AND PERFECTIONISM

Introduction

Please don't ever give me a plant. I promise you, I will kill it within three weeks. Its death won't be instant—plants seem to last without water about as long as a bunch of cut flowers. A friend of mine came to visit recently and saw a dying orchid on my table. "What's up with your plant?" she asked. I acknowledged that it was on its way out, which was no surprise since I never watered it. I suppose I could have gotten up at that point and watered it, but it seemed like a lot of effort.

My parents most definitely have green thumbs. I've always hoped that at some point those gifts would spring up within me, causing me to create botanical beauty all around. In fact, my husband and I bought an old farmhouse with two and a half acres in hopes that we'd come to love "tending the land." What we found is that we don't even like cutting the grass, let alone weeding and pruning a garden.

I'm a bit of an all-or-nothing person. If I can't do something well, I often don't even try. I settle for mediocrity. Yet in other areas of life I struggle with perfectionism. I can't stand when my toothpaste is squeezed in the middle instead of at the end, or when the dishwasher is loaded incorrectly, or when I fail to meet a deadline. Failure in an area of life that matters to me depresses me and makes me wonder why I bother trying at all.

My tendency to swing between mediocrity and perfectionism has always confused me a little bit, until I read a description of a "defeated perfectionist." This is a person who doesn't even want to get off the couch unless she's pretty certain she'll be successful at whatever she's endeavoring to do.

Wherever we fall on the spectrum (comfy in mediocrity, straining for perfection, or somewhere in between), God wants to make sure that we have a healthy, balanced attitude toward all that life requires. He wants us to experience the joy of stepping out and going wherever He calls us, without fear or trepidation.

Day One
DON'T SETTLE FOR MEDIOCRITY

God doesn't want us to float through life without direction or purpose. Our life is a journey with eternity at its end. In 2 Timothy 4:7–8, Saint Paul likened his life journey to a race: "I have competed well; I have finished the race; I have kept the faith. From now on the crown of righteousness awaits me, which the Lord, the just judge, will award to me on that day, and not only to me, but to all who have longed for his appearance." When we settle for mediocrity, we're unlikely to finish that race. We'll be less than who God created us to be. We'll settle for comfort and ease, but miss out on heavenly reward.

> The word mediocre is an interesting one; it comes from the Middle French term *mediocris* "in a middle state;" literally, "at middle height." It is a combination of *medi (us)* mid + OL *ocris* rugged mountain. In its most literal interpretation, it means "halfway up the mountain." What should be understood in this is that [we stop at the halfway point], and have no desire to go any further. It is not a matter of halfway on a continuing journey, but a contentment to be at the halfway point . . .[16]

Saint Paul never advocated settling halfway up the mountain. It's certainly not what Jesus modeled for us with His relentless pursuit of our salvation. We are to give our best to the One who gave everything He had for us.

1. What was Jesus' response to those who settle for mediocrity in Revelation 3:15, 16?

[16] Glendale Church of Christ, "Fighting the Good Fight: Fighting Mediocrity," Truth & Reason, September 15, 2013, http://www.truth-reason.com/wp-content/uploads/2013/09/ftgf6-fightingmediocrity.pdf.

2. What are followers of Christ called to in 1 Thessalonians 4:1, 9–10?

3. God knows we aren't going to arrive at the top of the mountain tomorrow. He sees that goal as a journey that takes a lifetime. What can you learn from Saint Paul's example in Philippians 3:12–14 regarding that journey?

4. What is your greater tendency—looking down the mountain and contenting yourself with how far you've come (while comparing yourself favorably with those who are farther down) or looking up the mountain with discouragement and a focus on your inadequacies? Have you sat down halfway up?

Quiet your heart and enjoy His presence. . . . He's calling you upward.

"Be eager to present yourself as acceptable to God, a workman who causes no disgrace, imparting the word of truth without deviation." (2 Timothy 2:15)

When we think our mediocre efforts to follow Christ are better than nothing, we often ignore the impact our actions have on others. Countless people are watching us. Our actions speak louder than our words, and Christians are being observed to see if God really does make a difference. When we claim to follow Christ but refuse to remain faithful when the road gets rocky and obedience is hard, people question whether we really are who we claim to be.

For your sake, as well as for the sake of those who are watching you, spend some time confessing any area of your life where you are settling for mediocrity. Remember, God doesn't expect you to attain the ideal immediately. He just wants you to faithfully continue on the journey. Every day offers a fresh opportunity to pursue excellence. And when we make mistakes, which we are bound to do, all we need to do is apologize, and start again tomorrow.

If we were to place mediocrity on one end of a spectrum, perfectionism would be at the other end. When either mediocrity or perfectionism is our standard way of operating, we fail to live balanced lives. Where does perfectionism come from? It's often rooted in a faulty self-image, unrealistic expectations, pride, or fear. We'll explore these roots of perfectionism during Days Two through Five.

Day Two
THE MEASURE OF SELF-WORTH

A faulty self-image can lead to perfectionism. How do you measure your worth? No matter where you go, you are continually receiving messages about what our culture says matters most. Airbrushed images of models cause you to make outward beauty the measure. Pinterest and HGTV tempt you to measure your worth by the perfection of your environment. The achievement-oriented culture tells you that your worth is measured by your accomplishments.

The checklist is long: Have a perfect body, perfect health, perfect clothes, have perfect relationships, achieve a perfect career, and consistently give back to those less fortunate. The result? Pressure, and a nagging sense that no matter what, you'll never be enough.

Author Richard Winter describes the consequence of living under this pressure:

> The core of the problem is that when a person's self worth depends on reaching those high standards, it is an inevitable script for self defeat and their own personal hell of repeated failure and eternal regret.[17]

If you wonder if your self-image is tied to these standards and measures, ask yourself the following:

Does my sense of worth fluctuate when I'm fifteen pounds overweight?

Does my sense of worth fluctuate depending on what I've accomplished in a day?

Would my sense of worth fluctuate if I had to downsize or scale back because of financial difficulties?

---

[17] Richard Winter, "Perfectionism: The Road to Heaven—or Hell?" L'Abri Papers, accessed March 3, 2014, http://www.labri.org/england/resources/05052008/RW01_Perfectionism.pdf.

God wants you to be freed from these faulty measures of your worth. He already measured your worth when Jesus hung on the cross, and He declared *you* worth dying for.

He loves you, and wants you to be rooted in that unconditional love. Perhaps you were loved conditionally in the past. God's love is different. Receiving and soaking up His unconditional love is the antidote to the bondage of trying to measure up to the perfect standard that the world says matters.

Sometimes it's hard to believe that you are treasured and loved by God. But you have to decide—whose voice are you going to listen to? Whom will you believe?

1. A. How did God prove His *unconditional* love for you? See Romans 5:8.

   B. What does that mean to you personally?

2. God speaks to you through the words of the prophet Jeremiah: "With age-old love I have loved you; so I have kept my mercy toward you. Again I will build you, and you shall stay built." (Jeremiah 31:3–4) This is a promise you can cling to. It is for you. He has loved you with an everlasting love, and He loves you too much to leave you as you are. He wants you to walk in freedom, totally transformed. He has fashioned all sorts of circumstances in your life to "build you" in this way. Some of those circumstances aren't the ones you would choose for yourself. Can you see any evidence, past or present, of God allowing difficulties into your life to build your character and strength? What should we remember from Jeremiah 29:11 when our circumstances tempt us to question God's love?

3. List the things that *cannot* separate us from the love of God according to Romans 8:31–39. Reread the list. Has one of those things made you feel as if you were separated from God's love? List it below. Will you believe the truth of God's word (nothing can separate you from His love) instead of what you may have felt in the past (or might be feeling right now)?

4. What does Psalm 139:13–16 say about the care God took when He created you?

Quiet your heart and enjoy His presence. . . . Base your self-worth on God's love for you.

Prayerfully read each of the following verses. Pause after each one and talk to God about any insights you've received.

"You alone, Lord, make me secure." (Psalm 4:9 NAB)

"Those who know your name trust in you; you never forsake those who seek you, Lord." (Psalm 9:11 NAB)

"He reached down from on high and seized me; drew me out of the deep waters. . . . He set me free in the open; he rescued me because he loves me." (Psalm 18:17, 20 NAB)

"You are my shelter." (Psalm 32:7)

"Though my flesh and my heart fail, God is the rock of my heart, my portion forever." (Psalm 73:26)

Day Three
CIRCLING BACK TO EXPECTATIONS

1. A. According to CCC 1776, each of us has an inner voice. Whose voice is this, and what does it call us to do? What is inscribed on each of our hearts?

   B. Have you ever experienced God speaking to you through your conscience? If so, describe it here.

2. It would be far easier to know what we should and shouldn't do if God's voice in our conscience were the only one we could hear. Unfortunately, our heads can become full of other voices, many coming from expectations of other people. It has been said that the way parents talk to their children becomes their children's inner voice. A child can equate a *parent's* approval or disapproval with *God's* approval or disapproval. When people are important to us, their expectations of us can become a litany we listen to whether they are speaking out loud or not. These voices compete for our attention and cause us confusion. Can you identify any expectations (think of the times you say "I should," "I must," or "I have to") that have become an inner voice, competing with God's voice within you?

Richard Winter describes the conscience of a perfectionist in the following way:

> Unhealthy perfectionists tend to have very sensitive and sometimes distorted consciences. They often feel acute pangs of guilt or shame if they do not live up to their own, or others', expectations. Fear about what others will think about their decisions and actions becomes their central concern.[18]

[18] Richard Winter, Perfecting Ourselves to Death: The Pursuit of Excellence and the Perils of Perfectionism (Downers Grove, IL: InterVarsity Press, 2005), 78.

3. We must accept the fact that we'll never measure up to the expectations of everyone around us. Nor should their approval be what we are pursuing. Our highest desire must be to please God. In order to know what He is asking of us, we need to quiet the voices of expectations so that we can hear God's voice echoing in the depths of our hearts. To quiet those voices, we have to be able to recognize them. Make a list of the expectations that pressure you, noting whom they come from. Cross out any expectations that are unrealistic during this season of your life.

4. A. We need to remember that no one understands us and our unique challenges and circumstances better than God. He asks only that we keep heading up the mountain, not that we arrive at its peak tomorrow. What do you learn from Psalm 103:13–14 regarding God's understanding of our limitations?

   B. How does God respond when we don't measure up to His expectations of us? See Psalm 103:8–12.

Quiet your heart and enjoy His presence. . . . A limitless supply of His grace is offered to you.

"Shame is a bully. Grace is a shield." —Ann Voskamp

We feel shame when we don't measure up to expectations. Shame bullies us, telling us that because we aren't perfectly meeting an external ideal, who we are *(not just what we do) is not good enough.*

God offers us grace as an antidote to shame. He knows that we fall short—He knows we are "of dust"—and He offers His grace to fill in the gap between who we are and who we want to be. God's grace covers us with His love.

If you can clear your head and heart of expectations, you'll be creating space for grace. *Take some time to prayerfully lay the expectations that press in on you at the foot of the cross. Release them to Jesus. The weight of sin's consequence fell on Him so it wouldn't fall on you. Look up at Jesus on the crucifix and remember what it cost Him so you could walk in grace.*

Day Four
THE PIT OF PRIDE

Pride is often at the root of a perfectionist's need to reach an unrealistically high standard with no mistakes allowed. We tend to picture pride as a person looking down his or her nose at someone else. That is one manifestation, but often it operates in a far subtler way. Pride causes us to desire control at all costs. Being limited by human weakness is incredibly frustrating to someone who struggles with pride. When a perfectionist focuses on her "inner checklist" of how to do everything perfectly, she hopes it will help to keep her life under control. It's hard for her to relinquish control to God, but it's her only hope of living in freedom.

1. How is faith defined in Hebrews 11:1?

2. Faith is how we handle what we cannot see. A perfectionist who struggles with pride dislikes unpredictability. She wants to control potential outcomes so she can keep it all together. The first step for her to break free of pride's grip is to recognize that the only control she'll ever gain will be an *illusion* of control. Life, by definition, is unpredictable and full of uncertainty. Like it or not, you are not in control of your own destiny. There is much you can do to shape it, but ultimately, there are things you cannot predict or change. Who *is* in control? See Psalm 31:15–16.

3. We can try to control our lives (pride), or we can live out the truth of Psalm 28:7. Read this verse, and record what it means to you personally. Think of a specific area of life that you wish you could perfectly control. Apply this verse to that situation.

4. We will feel pride loosen its grip in direct proportion to how much we trust God. According to Psalm 9:11 NAB, who is able to trust God?

In the Bible, a person's name reveals something about his or her character. Knowing God's name means that we know who He is. The more we know Him, the better we'll be able to trust Him.

Quiet your heart and enjoy His presence. . . . God is God. You are not. And that's a good thing.

We cannot control everything, because we are not God. We can control a lot more than our ancestors did, but there will always be a gap between what we'd like to control and what is out of our hands. The more we trust God, the easier this will be to accept. Read the following Hebrew names of God and their descriptions. Which name reveals something about God that helps you trust Him? Pray to Him using that name. Ask Him to give you more faith to believe in what you cannot see.

El Shaddai (Genesis 17:1): All-sufficient one, Lord God almighty

Jehovah-Rapha (Exodus 15:26): The Lord who heals

Yahweh-yireh (Genesis 22:14): The Lord who provides

Jehovah Mekoddishkem (Exodus 31:13): The Lord who sanctifies you

Jehovah Shalom (Judges 6:24): The Lord is peace

Jehovah Raah (Psalm 23): The Lord my shepherd

Day Five
THE GRIP OF FEAR

If we were to peel back the top layer of perfectionism, we would find fear underneath.

1. A common fear that drives a perfectionist's behavior is the fear of failure. Failing to perfectly accomplish goals can feel like failing as a person. Underneath that fear is a deep desire to be unconditionally loved and accepted, but it's hard for the perfectionist to believe that love doesn't have to be earned. What wisdom and comfort can be gained from Isaiah 43:1–2 when fearing failure?

2. Isaiah 43:1 says that God has redeemed us. The word *redemption* means atonement for a fault or mistake; rescue; deliverance.[19] What purchased our redemption? See 1 Peter 1:18–19 (note: some translations of this verse use the word *redeemed*; others use *ransomed*).

It's important to note that our "perfect" behavior is not what has purchased our redemption. Our faults and mistakes aren't atoned for because we manage to work extra hard and almost always get things right. In Ephesians 1:7, Saint Paul writes, "In him we have redemption by his blood, the forgiveness of transgressions, in accord with the riches of his grace that he lavished upon us." God has planned ahead for our failure. Nothing surprises Him. Even the most colossal personal failure will not place us out of reach of redemption. Redemption, forgiveness, and grace are always offered to us.

3. Because of the desire to control things and not make mistakes, perfectionists can fear commitment. Procrastination in decision making is common because perfectionists want to be absolutely certain of which decision is most likely to bring the desired outcome. What should be our first step in decision making? How is an indecisive man (a man of two minds) described in James 1:5–8?

[19] Dictionary.com, s. v. "redemption," http://dictionary.reference.com/browse/redemption.

4. What does God promise to do for us if we love Him? How might this truth impact our willingness to make decisions even when we can't be guaranteed of the outcome? See Romans 8:28.

While we are wise to think and pray before we act, at some point a leap of faith is often required. "But what if I've made the wrong choice?" the perfectionist cries. Richard Winter describes the perfectionist's motto as "Nothing ventured, nothing lost."[20] While procrastinating may seem like the safest way to behave, what we actually lose is the opportunity to learn from our mistakes. This is one of God's favorite ways to teach us. Our mistakes don't derail Him. He uses them for our good.

Quiet your heart and enjoy His presence. . . . He is greater than anything we fear.

When we aren't sure of the perfect way to go forward but we have prayed and asked for God's direction, we can pray the following:

Dear Lord,

I'm stepping forward in this particular direction. I've drawn on the wisdom of my past experiences and the things you've taught me through Scripture and the teachings of the Church. If this course of action is not the direction you want me to go in but I didn't hear you clearly, I pray you will teach me something through my mistake. I am going to walk through this door, and I pray that you would close it before I get there if it isn't your will."

Conclusion

Since only one day was devoted to mediocrity and the perfectionists were the focus of four solid days, I think something nice should be said about those overachievers with the high blood pressure. **Perfectionists are right to long for the perfect.** When they identify and want the ideal, they are revealing the need for things to be made right. The confusion lies in where and when that perfection is going to occur.

---

[20] Winter, "Perfectionism."

Here's the deal: It's not going to happen here. We'll experience perfection in heaven. In the meantime, we have to learn to deal with the not quite, the less than perfect, the could be better, and the downright irritating.

"Wait a minute," the overachieving perfectionist says. She's been working overtime (she's good at that) and has found a verse in her Bible that we did not talk about this week. And she thinks it bears a little discussion since Jesus is the one who said it: "Be perfect, just as your heavenly Father is perfect." (Matthew 5:48)

She's feeling pretty good about this discovery, because Jesus did not say, "Wait and do this when you get to heaven."

Before you panic and think that everything we studied this week is being debunked, we're going to unpack the word *perfect*. In the original Greek, the word is *teleios*, which means "mature . . . going through the necessary stages to reach the end-goal, i.e. developed into a consummating completion by fulfilling the necessary process (spiritual journey). . . . It is well-illustrated with the old pirate's telescope, unfolding (extending out) one stage at a time to function at full-strength."[21] We are called to maturity and holiness. We are in the process of being transformed. It's a journey.

During this journey toward our ultimate goal—total spiritual maturity and transformation—we rely on the merits and perfection of Christ.

The cross is the great equalizer. We all come there with empty hands. We acknowledge that we're all in equal need of God's grace. Even if we've got more good works compiled than another person, we still fall short of God's requirement of perfect holiness. No matter whom we are talking about—Saint Thomas Aquinas, Saint Teresa of Calcutta, you or me—there is a gap between the best we've got and the holiness that God requires for us to spend eternity with Him. We can't be perfect. We will always fall short. ("For all have sinned and are deprived of the glory of God." [Romans 3:23]) He took the punishment that was due us, and filled in the gap between us and God. Jesus came, and He *was* and *is* perfect, and He stood in our place.

> "I'm not relying on my own merits, as I have none, but I put my hope in Him who is goodness and holiness Himself. It is He alone who, satisfied with my feeble efforts, will raise me to Him, will clothe me with His infinite merits, and will make me a saint."[22] —Saint Thérèse of Lisieux

---

[21] Bible Hub, s. v. "teleios," accessed March 6, 2014, http://biblehub.com/greek/5046.htm.
[22] St. Thérèse of Lisieux, *The Story of a Soul* (New York: Doubleday, 2001), 37–38.

My Resolution

In what specific way will I apply what I learned in this lesson?

Examples:

1. I'll rise above the level of mediocrity by setting my alarm thirty minutes earlier than normal and spending time in prayer. Instead of procrastinating the tasks I least like, I will do them *first.*

2. In order to break free from measuring my self-worth by the external standards of our culture, I will stand under "the shower of God's love." I'll do this by writing down the Bible verses studied during Day Two that meant the most to me, and read them throughout the day.

3. I will make a decision this week that I have been vacillating over. Instead of making the decision in a spirit of fear, I will make it in the spirit of faith, knowing that even if the result is not the one I hope for, God can and will work through all of my circumstances, even those caused by my mistakes.

My Resolution:

Catechism Clips

CCC 1776 "Deep within his conscience man discovers a law which he has not laid upon himself but which he must obey. Its voice, ever calling him to love and to do what is good and to avoid evil, sounds in his heart at the right moment. . . . For man has in his heart a law inscribed by God. . . . His conscience is man's most secret core and his sanctuary. There he is alone with God whose voice echoes in his depths."

Verse Study

See Appendix 2 for instructions on how to complete a verse study.

2 Corinthians 3:18

1. Verse:

2. Paraphrase:

3. Questions:

4. Cross-references:

5. Personal Application:

NOTES

Appendices

NOTES

Appendix 1
SAINT THÉRÈSE OF LISIEUX

Patron Saint of Walking with Purpose

Saint Thérèse of Lisieux was gifted with the ability to take the riches of our Catholic faith and explain them in a way that a child could imitate. The wisdom she gleaned from Scripture ignited a love in her heart for her Lord that was personal and transforming. The simplicity of the faith that she laid out in her writings is so completely Catholic that Pope Pius XII said, "She rediscovered the Gospel itself, the very heart of the Gospel."

Walking with Purpose is intended to be a means by which women can honestly share their spiritual struggles and embark on a journey that is refreshing to the soul. It was never intended to facilitate the deepest of intellectual study of Scripture. Instead, the focus has been to help women know Christ: to know His heart, to know His tenderness, to know His mercy, and to know His love. Our logo is a little flower, and that has meaning. When a woman begins to open her heart to God, it's like the opening of a little flower. It can easily be bruised or crushed, and it must be treated with the greatest of care. Our desire is to speak to women's hearts no matter where they are in life, baggage and all, and gently introduce truths that can change their lives.

Saint Thérèse of Lisieux, the little flower, called her doctrine "the little way of spiritual childhood," and it is based on complete and unshakable confidence in God's love for us. She was not introducing new truths. She spent countless hours reading Scripture and she shared what she found, emphasizing the importance of truths that had already been divinely revealed. We can learn so much from her:

> The good God would not inspire unattainable desires; I can, then, in spite of my littleness, aspire to sanctity. For me to become greater is impossible; I must put up with myself just as I am with all my imperfections. But I wish to find the way to go to Heaven by a very straight, short, completely new little way. We are in a century of inventions: now one does not even have to take the trouble to climb the steps of a stairway; in the homes of the rich, an elevator replaces them nicely. I, too, would like to find an elevator to lift me up to Jesus, for I am too little to climb the rough stairway of perfection. So I have looked in the

books of the saints for a sign of the elevator I long for, and I have read these words proceeding from the mouth of eternal Wisdom: "He that is a little one, let him turn to me" (Proverbs 9:16). So I came, knowing that I had found what I was seeking, and wanting to know, O my God, what You would do with the little one who would answer Your call, and this is what I found:

"As one whom the mother caresses, so will I comfort you. You shall be carried at the breasts and upon the knees they shall caress you" (Isaiah 66:12–13). Never have more tender words come to make my soul rejoice. The elevator which must raise me to the heavens is Your arms, O Jesus! For that I do not need to grow; on the contrary, I must necessarily remain small, become smaller and smaller. O my God, You have surpassed what I expected, and I want to sing Your mercies. (Saint Thérèse of the Infant Jesus, *Histoire d'une Ame: Manuscrits Autobiographiques* [Paris: Éditions du Seuil, 1998], 244.)

Appendix 2
HOW TO DO A VERSE STUDY

A verse study is an exciting Bible study tool that can help to bring the Scriptures to life! By reading, reflecting on, and committing a verse to memory, we open ourselves to the Holy Spirit, who reveals very personal applications of our Lord's words and actions to our daily lives.

Learning to do a verse study is not difficult, but it can be demanding. In this Walking with Purpose™ study, a Bible verse has been selected to reinforce a theme of each lesson. To do the verse study, read the verse and then follow these simple instructions. You'll be on your way to a deeper and more personal understanding of Scripture.

- **Read the verse and the paragraph before and after the verse.**

- **Write out the selected verse.**

- **Paraphrase.**
  Write the verse using your own words. What does the verse say?

- **Ask questions.**
  Write down any questions you have about the verse. What does it say that you don't understand?

- **Use cross-references.**
  Look up other Bible verses that help to shed light on what the selected verse means. A study Bible will often list cross-references in the margin or in the study notes. Another excellent resource is Biblos.com. This website allows you to enter a specific Bible verse and it will provide many cross-references and additional insights into the passage of Scripture you selected. Record any insights you gain from the additional verses you are able to find.

- **Make a personal application.**
  What does the verse say to you personally? Is there a promise to make? a warning to heed? an example to follow? Ask God to help you find something from the verse that you can apply to your life.

The recommended Bible translations for use in Walking with Purpose™ studies are: The New American Bible, which is the translation used in the United States for the readings at Mass; The Revised Standard Version, Catholic Edition; and The Jerusalem Bible.

A SAMPLE VERSE STUDY

1. **Verse:**
   John 15:5 "I am the vine, you are the branches. Those who abide in me and I in them bear much fruit, because apart from me you can do nothing."

2. **Paraphrase:**
   Jesus is the vine, I am the branch. If I abide in Him, then I'll be fruitful, but if I try to do everything on my own, I'll fail at what matters most. I need Him.

3. **Questions:**
   What does it mean to abide? How does Jesus abide in me? What kind of fruit is Jesus talking about?

4. **Cross-references:**
   John 6:56 "He that eats my flesh, and drinks my blood, abides in me, and I in him." This verse brings to mind the Eucharist, and the importance of receiving Christ in the Eucharist as often as possible. This is a very important way to abide in Jesus.

   John 15:7 "If you abide in me, and my words abide in you, ask for whatever you wish, and it will be done for you." How can Jesus' words abide in me if I never read them? I need to read the Bible if I want to abide in Christ.

   John 15:16 "It was not you who chose me, but I who chose you and appointed you to go and bear fruit that will remain, so that whatever you ask the Father in my name he may give you." Not all fruit remains. Some is good only temporarily—on earth. I want my fruit to remain in eternity—to count in the long run.

   Galatians 5:22–23 "The fruit of the Spirit is love, joy, peace, patience, kindness, generosity, faithfulness, gentleness, self-control." These are some of the fruits that will be seen if I abide in Christ.

5. **Personal Application:**
   I will study my calendar this week, making note of where I spend my time. Is most of my time spent on things that will last for eternity (fruit that remains)? I'll reassess my priorities in light of what I find.

NOTES

Appendix 3
CONVERSION OF HEART

The Catholic faith is full of beautiful traditions, rituals, and sacraments. As powerful as they are, it is possible for them to become mere habits in our lives, instead of experiences that draw us close to the heart of Christ. In the words of John Paul II, they can become acts of "hollow ritualism." We might receive our first Communion and the sacraments of confession and confirmation, yet never experience the interior conversion that opens the heart to a personal relationship with God.

Pope Benedict XVI has explained that the "door of faith" is opened at one's baptism, but we are called to open it again, walk through it, and rediscover and renew our relationship with Christ and His Church.[23]

So how do we do this? How do we walk through that door of faith so we can begin to experience the abundant life that God has planned for us?

GETTING PERSONAL

The word *conversion* means "the act of turning." This means that conversion involves a turning away from one thing and a turning toward another. When you haven't experienced conversion of heart, you are turned *toward* your own desires. You are the one in charge, and you do what you feel is right and best at any given moment. You may choose to do things that are very good for other people, but the distinction is that *you are choosing*. You are deciding. You are the one in control.

Imagine driving a car. You are sitting in the driver's seat, and your hands are on the steering wheel. You've welcomed Jesus into the passenger's seat, and have listened to His comments. But whether or not you follow His directions is really up to you. You may follow them or you may not, depending on what seems right to you.

When you experience interior conversion, you decide to turn, to get out of the driver's seat, move into the passenger's seat, and invite God to be the driver. Instead of seeing Him as an advice giver or someone nice to have around for the holidays, you give Him control of every aspect of your life.

More than likely, you don't find this easy to do. This is because of the universal struggle with pride. We want to be the ones in charge. We don't like to be in

[23] Pope Benedict XVI, *Apostolic Letter: Porta Fidei*, for the Indiction of the Year of Faith, October 11, 2011.

desperate need. We like to be the captains of our ships, charting our own courses. As William Ernest Henley wrote, "I am the master of my fate: I am the captain of my soul."

Conversion of heart isn't possible without humility. The first step is to recognize your desperate need of a savior. Romans 6:23 states that the "wages of sin is death." When you hear this, you might be tempted to justify your behavior, or compare yourself with others. You might think to yourself, "I'm not a murderer. I'm not as bad as this or that person. If someone were to put my good deeds and bad deeds on a scale, my good ones would outweigh the bad. So surely I am good enough? Surely I don't deserve death!" When this is your line of thought, you are missing a very important truth: Just one mortal sin is enough to separate you from a holy God. Just one mortal sin is enough for you to deserve death.[24] Even your best efforts to do good fall short of what God has required in order for you to spend eternity with Him. Isaiah 64:6 says, "All our righteous acts are like filthy rags." If you come to God thinking that you are going to be accepted by Him based on your "good conduct," He will point out that your righteousness is nothing compared to His infinite holiness.

Saint Thérèse of Lisieux understood this well, and wrote, "In the evening of my life I shall appear before You with empty hands, for I do not ask You to count my works. All our justices are stained in Your eyes. I want therefore to clothe myself in Your own justice and receive from Your love the eternal possession of Yourself."[25]

She recognized that her works, her best efforts, wouldn't be enough to earn salvation. Salvation cannot be earned. It's a free gift. Saint Thérèse accepted this gift, and said that if her justices or righteous deeds were stained, then she wanted to clothe herself in Christ's own justice. We see this described in 2 Corinthians 5:21: "God made him who had no sin to be sin for us, so that in him we might become the righteousness of God."

How did God make Him who had no sin to be sin for you? This was foretold by the prophet Isaiah: "But he was pierced for our transgressions, he was crushed for our iniquities; the punishment that brought us peace was upon him, and by his wounds we are healed" (Isaiah 53:5).

---

[24] One sin was enough to merit death for the first human beings who were in the state of preternatural perfection. For us, joined to Christ in His Body, one mortal sin merits death. Venial sin does not, although venial sin makes it easier to commit mortal sin. See CCC #1854-#1864.

[25] Saint Thérèse of Lisieux, "Act of Oblation to Merciful Love," June 9, 1895.

Jesus accomplished this on the cross. Every sin committed, past, present, and future, was placed on Him. Now, *all the merits of Jesus can be yours.* He wants to fill your empty hands with His own virtues.

But first, you need to recognize, just as Saint Thérèse did, that you are little. You are weak. You fail. You need forgiveness. You need a savior.

When you come before God in prayer and acknowledge these truths, He looks at your heart. He sees your desire to trust Him, to please Him, to obey Him. He says to you, "My precious child, you don't have to pay for your sins. My Son, Jesus, has already done that for you. He suffered, so that you wouldn't have to. I want to experience a relationship of intimacy with you. I forgive you.[26] Jesus came to set you free.[27] When you open your heart to me, you become a new creation![28] The old you has gone. The new you is here. If you will stay close to me, and journey by my side, you will begin to experience a transformation that brings joy and freedom.[29] I've been waiting to pour my gifts into your soul. Beloved daughter of mine, remain confident in me. I am your loving Father. Crawl into my lap. Trust me. Love me. I will take care of everything."

This is conversion of heart. This act of faith lifts the veil from your eyes and launches you into the richest and most satisfying life. You don't have to be sitting in church to do this. Don't let a minute pass before opening your heart to God and inviting Him to come dwell within you. Let Him sit in the driver's seat. Give Him the keys to your heart. Your life will never be the same again.

---

[26] "If we acknowledge our sins, he is faithful and just and will forgive our sins and cleanse us from every wrongdoing." 1 John 1:9

[27] "So if the Son makes you free, you will be free indeed." John 8:36

[28] "So whoever is in Christ is a new creation: the old things have passed away; behold, new things have come." 2 Corinthians 5:18

[29] "I will sprinkle clean water over you to make you clean; from all your impurities and from all your idols I will cleanse you. I will give you a new heart, and a new spirit I will put within you. I will remove the heart of stone from your flesh and give you a heart of flesh." Ezekiel 36:25–26

NOTES

Answer Key

NOTES

Lesson 1, Day One

1. Shame.
2. The devil planted a seed of doubt in Eve's heart by saying, "Did God *really* say . . . ?" Then he called God a liar. God had said that if they ate from the tree of knowledge of good and evil they would die. The devil said, "You certainly will not die!" He then went on to describe God as holding back on Eve, accusing Him of not wanting Eve's eyes to be opened.
3. The hiding began after Adam and Eve sinned and realized that they were naked. The root cause was sin, and the accompanying feeling that they were no longer worthy of connection to God and His love.
4. Genesis 3:15 is known as the "protoevangelium," or the first mention of the gospel. In this verse, God said that "the woman's offspring" (Jesus) would be struck on the heel by the devil (a painful blow), but that Jesus would strike a mortal blow to the devil's head.

Lesson 1, Day Two

1. John 8:44 tells us that the devil "was a murderer from the beginning and does not stand in truth because there is no truth in him. When he tells a lie, he speaks in character, because he is a liar and the father of lies."
2. If we remain in God's Word (the Bible), we will recognize truth, and be set free.
3. Scripture is living. This makes it far more powerful than any self-help book. It's effective. It effectively teaches truth that can guide our lives and remind us of God's infinite love for us. It's able to penetrate between soul and spirit, joints and marrow. It can speak to our hearts with laser-like accuracy, convicting us about areas of needed change or giving just the right words of comfort.
4. It's described as a spiritual battle. Our weapons are not of flesh, but they are enormously powerful—*strong* enough to destroy a fortress. Our weapons are strong enough to destroy the arguments and pretensions that the devil speaks to us. We can take every thought captive in obedience to Christ. We are not slaves to our thoughts. We can take charge, through God's power, and think about the right and true things.

Lesson 1, Day Three

1. God's power isn't made perfect in us when we are performing at our optimal level. That's not what this Scripture says. It says that God's power is made perfect when we are weak. When all we can offer God is empty hands and failure, He says, "I'm so glad that I have the opportunity to show you that I am enough."
2. Romans 5:8 teaches us that God didn't wait until we were all cleaned up and perfect to show His love by dying for us. He died for us when we were a mess. In Ephesians 2:4–9 we are reminded that God brought us to life with Christ because of His great love, not our great perfection. We have been saved through grace. This is His gift to us; it is unearned. It is based not on the worth of our works, but on His work on our behalf.
3. God doesn't determine our worth by our weight or what we look like. He looks into our hearts and loves what He sees there. He created us as His beloved daughters, and He doesn't make mistakes. You are His masterpiece. You are beautiful in His eyes!
4. From the moment of your conception, you were seen and valued by God. He cares about you, thinks about you, surrounds you, and rests His loving hand on you. There is

nowhere you can go where He won't follow. He'll even follow you into the darkness, and will shed light on your path so you can come back to the daylight.

Lesson 1, Day Four

1. Busyness and distractions make it hard for us to take the time to process hurt. When we don't like conflict, another layer of complexity is added. We'll often deny hurt in order to avoid having to discuss it with the person who has wounded us. Expectations regarding the way we should behave can come from family of origin or religious teaching. Many of us believe that a gracious woman doesn't get angry and so we stuff those feelings instead of expressing them in a healthy way.
2. If we delight ourselves in the Lord, He will give us the desires of our heart.
3. Answers will vary.
4. Answers will vary.

Lesson 1, Day Five

1. Our "light must shine before others" because of our good works. This will bring glory to God. We are to "live in a manner worthy of the call we've received." We are to relate to one another with humility, gentleness, and patience, bearing with one another through love and striving to preserve unity. We're to live in such a way that even if people speak negatively about us, our good works will be seen and will speak for themselves, bringing glory to God. In this, your integrity will silence the ignorance of foolish people.
2. The precepts of the Lord (found in Scripture) show us what is right. God's commands are clear, and enlighten us when we're discerning what we should do. God's Word can serve as a lamp for our feet, showing us which way to go. The Bible isn't just words written by humans; it's actually God's words. It's how He talks to us (CCC 104). Scriptures teach us what is true. They are without error, and utterly trustworthy (CCC 107).
3. People can sense when our motives are impure. We aren't to do things so that people notice us. We are to do all that we do in order to bring glory to God, not ourselves.
4. Jesus says that if we bring our gift to the altar (a description of worship) and remember that a brother has something against us, we are to go and be reconciled before offering the gift.

Lesson 2, Day One

1. **Revelation 4:11** God is worthy of being our highest priority because He is our Creator. If He hadn't willed it, none of us would exist. He sustains our every breath simply because He wants to. "In his hand is the soul of every living thing, and the life breath of all mortal flesh." (Job 12:10)

   John 3:16 Out of love for us, God sent His only Son to die in our place. He didn't wait for us to clean up and to be "good enough" to warrant such sacrifice. "While we were still sinners, Christ died for us." (Romans 5:8) He gave us the greatest gift possible when we were completely undeserving, simply because He loves us.
2. If we don't put God first, we'll replace Him with something else. Whatever we put in the place of God becomes an idol. This means we'll "become slaves to things that by nature are not gods." (Galatians 4:8) Christ died on the cross and set us free so we could

experience true freedom. If we become enslaved again, it is by our own choice. It's because we've allowed something else to take the place of God in our lives. If we don't make God the first priority in our lives, we risk becoming slaves again.

3. Answers will vary.

Lesson 2, Day Two

1. Jesus said that the second-greatest commandment is "loving your neighbor as yourself."
2. Answers will vary.
3. Answers will vary.
4. Answers will vary.

Lesson 2, Day Three

1. **A.** Every single baptized Christian is God's child, and receives at least one spiritual gift. No one gets skipped.
  B. The source of those gifts is the indwelling Holy Spirit. He distributes them "individually to each person as he wishes," (1 Corinthians 12:11) which means that we don't get to choose. God knows exactly what each of us needs in order to fulfill our God-given purpose and passion.
2. The spiritual gifts (also referred to as "charisms") listed in 1 Corinthians 12:8–10 are wisdom, knowledge, faith, healing, miracles (mighty deeds), prophecy, discernment of spirits, tongues, and interpretation of tongues.
3. Spiritual gifts are given to us by God so that we can serve *others*. They are to be used to advance God's purposes, not our own. They are to bring honor to God, not fame to ourselves. They are to build up and benefit the Church, and help meet the world's needs.

Lesson 2, Day Four

1. **A.** **2 Corinthians 4:17** says that our difficulties are "momentary light afflictions" and they are producing for us an eternal weight of glory beyond all comparison.
  B. **Romans 5:4** says that "affliction produces endurance, and endurance, proven character, and proven character, hope."
2. It says that we should fix our eyes not on what is seen but on what is unseen, because what is seen is transitory, but what is unseen is eternal.
3. We are being watched and surrounded by a great crowd of witnesses.
4. They are watching us run the race that lies before us.
5. Answers will vary.
Answers will vary.

Lesson 2, Day Five

1. While it was still dark, Jesus got up early to pray. His prayer life allowed Him to gain clarity in terms of the things that His Father wanted Him to say and to do. He didn't respond to every need. Much remained undone. But He always did His Father's will. He allowed God to set His priorities. "His words and works are the visible manifestation of his prayer in secret." (CCC 2602)
2. Answers will vary.
3. Answers will vary.

4. Answers will vary.

Lesson 3, Day One

1. Answers will vary.
2. Jesus never promised that this balance would be easy. In fact, He said there would be times when we'd need to choose Him over family, and that is painful. When Jesus spelled out the cost of putting Him first, He recognized that this was a cross to bear. He knows this obedience isn't easy. He also promised that there would be a reward. When we experience loss in our lives for His sake, we can be assured that God will not be outdone in generosity. "Whoever loses his life for my sake will find it." (Matthew 10:39) We find true life, eternal life, in Christ alone.
3. The sacraments are a conduit of God's grace and love. God loves nothing more than pouring out His presence, His love, and His mercy. In addition, He waits every day for us to turn our hearts to Him in prayer. No matter where we are, we can turn our focus to Him, asking Him to bathe us in His love. Reading Scripture helps to renew our thinking. We have so many false messages playing in our minds. When we read the Bible, we begin to replace the lies with the truth. The truth is, God loves you. Nothing you can do will diminish or take away that love. Regardless of how disappointed the people around you might be, when you come to God, He is never disappointed. He's just thrilled that you came.

Lesson 3, Day Two

1. Answers will vary.
2. Answers will vary.
3. **Matthew 9:10–13** He draws near to us to offer us healing.
   1 John 1:9 He forgives our sins and gives us a fresh start.
   Matthew 11:28–30 He takes the burden of perfectionism off our shoulders, and replaces it with His yoke.
4. Answers will vary.

Lesson 3, Day Three

1. Answers will vary.
2. **Isaiah 43:2** When we are going through periods of suffering and feel as if we are going under, God will hold our heads above water. We may feel as if our circumstances are going to get the better of us, but God promises us that if we lean on Him, we will not be consumed.
   2 Corinthians 12:9–10 and **Hebrews 13:5** Even when we are feeling the hardships and constraints that come from financial pressure, God will stand in the gap and provide us with strength to endure. When we are struggling financially, we feel weak and vulnerable. This verse reminds us that when we are weakest, God's strength is powerful enough. His strength is sufficient to get us through whatever we face. God promises that He will never forsake or abandon us, and encourages us to be content with what we have.
   Psalm 139:1–10 God knows us completely because He made us, and He never leaves us. There is nowhere we can go that is out of His reach. He is behind us, before us, resting His hand on us. His right hand holds us fast. We may not feel it, but He is there.

Psalm 23:4 Even when we are facing death, we don't need to fear, because God is with us. Death takes us to a place where no loved one can accompany us. But God is there.

3. The core issue is trust. This was Adam and Eve's undoing. They let their trust in their Creator die, and as a result, disobeyed God. When we lack trust in God, we are at great risk. The next step is the abuse of our freedom (our free will), and sin is the inevitable consequence.

Lesson 3, Day Four

1. We are to display compassion, kindness, lowliness, meekness, patience, forgiveness, and love. All of this should be the outward evidence of our inner peace.
2. Answers will vary.
3. Answers will vary.
4. Answers will vary.
5. **Joshua 24:15** Alternative response: "I *can* help how I react. I have a choice. I'm responsible for my choice. I can choose whom I'm going to serve. I am not going to serve my expectations. I'm going to serve God and respond to my disappointment graciously."

   Philippians 4:13 Alternative response: "I *can* control my emotions. I can do all things through Christ. His Holy Spirit dwells in me, and the power of the Spirit is stronger than my most intense emotions."

   2 Corinthians 12:9 Alternative response: "I *can* take it, and I *will* persevere. I choose to step out in God's power, which shows itself perfect when I am at my weakest."

Lesson 3, Day Five

1. Mary and Joseph expected that when their caravan left Jerusalem, Jesus would come along with the group. Families traveled in large "companies" and looked out for one another's children, which explains why Mary and Joseph didn't immediately notice Jesus' absence. When they found Him, Jesus asked them why they wouldn't have expected Him to be in His heavenly Father's house. He obediently returned home with them, but made it clear that His heavenly Father was to be obeyed before anyone else.
2. James and John expected Jesus to come into power, and they figured their closeness to Him should win them each places of honor in the new kingdom. Jesus encouraged them to adjust their expectations. Their association with Him wouldn't earn them seats of honor in Israel; rather, it would earn them the place of suffering servants.
3. The people expected Jesus to bring them political relief. They had been under the rule of the Roman government, and wanted a savior who brought more than spiritual freedom. When the people wanted to make Him king, Jesus did not succumb to the temptation of power and fame. Instead, He slipped away into the hills by Himself.
4. Answers will vary.

Lesson 4, Day One

1. God said that it isn't good for people to be alone. The first relationship He created was totally authentic and vulnerable. Adam and Eve "were both naked, yet they felt no shame." We were made to be in community, complementing one another in our differences and helping each other in our need.

2. "Trustworthy are the blows of a friend" refers to words from a friend that hurt but are valuable because they are spoken in love for our good. "Kisses of an enemy" are dangerous. An enemy doesn't desire our best. An enemy doesn't see our potential and challenge us to reach for holiness. "Iron sharpens iron" means that we can learn so much from one another when we are in authentic relationship. When we really care about someone, sometimes we need to speak the truth in love. This should always be done with gentleness, but often, even truth gently put is a blow. We are wise, though, when we consider the spirit in which the words are spoken and embrace any truth in those words.
3. We need encouragement, people who will pick us up when we fall down. We're told to bear one another's burdens. We weren't meant to go it alone.
4. Answers will vary.

Lesson 4, Day Two

1. **A.** We are to bear one another's burdens and to carry our own load.
   B. Answers will vary.
2. You need to see *fruit* of repentance—not just *words* of repentance.
3. Answers will vary.
4. We read in 2 Corinthians 9:7 that God wants us to give without sadness or compulsion. He wants us to give cheerfully. According to 1 John 4:18, "perfect love casts out fear." When our motive is fear, our actions are tainted. God wants us to cheerfully give for the right reasons and at the right times.

Lesson 4, Day Three

1. Answers will vary.
2. We should try to look at the situation from the other person's perspective, and try to give him or her the benefit of the doubt. Asking questions to clarify the person's words or actions is very helpful. If it becomes clear that he or she truly is at fault and the matter needs to be discussed, it should be done one-on-one with that person.
3. If the person doesn't listen, we are to take one or two other people along and address the issue again.
4. Our words should be pure (free from ill motive), peaceful, gentle, and sincere.

Lesson 4, Day Four

1. Answers will vary.
2. We are to put away falsehood and speak the truth. It's not a sin to be angry, but we need to watch what we say when we're angry. Evil talk shouldn't come out of our mouths, but just the things that are helpful for building others up. Our words should bring grace to those who hear them. Bitterness, wrath, anger, clamor, and slander shouldn't be found in our talk. Those things should be replaced with kindness and forgiveness.
3. Answers will vary.
4. Our words come from what is stored up in our hearts. We need help on the heart level in order to speak differently. It isn't enough to improve our communication skills. We need our hearts to be changed. We need *new hearts*, and this is exactly what God promises to provide.

Lesson 4, Day Five

1. Saint Paul prayed that we would know the **hope** that belongs to the call of Christ.
2. We receive the **riches** of glory.
3. God makes His power available to those who believe.
4. Answers will vary.

Lesson 5, Day One

1. Jesus said He would rather people be hot or cold than lukewarm. He said that He would spit the lukewarm out of His mouth.
2. We are called to take the instructions we've received in terms of how we are to behave, and then do them even more. Instead of settling for mediocrity, we are urged to "progress even more."
3. Paul knew that he hadn't attained perfect maturity, but he didn't let that discourage him to the point that he would quit trying. He continued his pursuit in hopes that he one day would reach that place. Instead of looking back, he pressed forward with his eyes fixed on what lay ahead. He relentlessly continued the pursuit of the heavenly prize.
4. Answers will vary.

Lesson 5, Day Two

1. **A.** God proved His love for us in that while we were still sinners, Christ died for us. He didn't wait until we had cleaned ourselves up or gotten back on track. He considered us worth everything when we were at our sinful worst.
   B. Answers will vary.
2. God's plans for us are for our good. When He allows difficult circumstances, He knows that they can benefit us somehow, some way. The blessing hidden in the pain may be hard to find, and if we're honest, we don't always find the blessing equals the loss. Sometimes we can see good come from a circumstance, but what we lost was worth more to us than that good. This is where we need to trust God's greater perspective on life. He sees the past, present, and future. He knows better than we do what is best for us in the long run.
3. Other people condemning us cannot separate us from Christ's love. Anguish, distress, persecution, famine, nakedness, peril, or the sword cannot separate us from God's love. Death, life, angels, principalities, present things, future things, powers, height, depth, nor any person can separate us from God's love.
4. It says that He formed your inmost being and knit you together in your mother's womb. Even before she knew you, God knew you. God saw you, unformed, and created you as a masterpiece. You are not a mistake. The *way* God made you is not a mistake. He made a plan for you; your days were shaped, even before one of them came to be. You are precious to God.

Lesson 5, Day Three

1. **A.** It is God's voice. He speaks to us deep within our conscience. He calls us to love and to do what is good and to avoid evil. God's law is inscribed on each of our hearts.
   B. Answers will vary.
2. Answers will vary.

3. Answers will vary.
4. **A.** He looks at us with compassion. He knows we're "of dust"—that we are only human, with limitations and circumstances that challenge us.
   B. He responds with mercy, and removes our sin from us when we ask for forgiveness. He separates us from our sin as far as the east is from the west.

Lesson 5, Day Four

1. Faith is the realization of things we have hoped for and the evidence of things not seen.
2. God is in control of your destiny.
3. God is our strength and shield. I don't want to be weak or to have limitations. When I can't perfectly and tirelessly accomplish all I aim to do, I become frustrated with my weaknesses. My weakness can be either a source of discouragement or a reminder that when I am weak, God is my strength. His Holy Spirit is within me, and strengthens me when I can't go on. I also want to control things so that nothing bad happens to me or to those I love. When I remember that God is my shield, I remember that I don't need to be the shield, protecting everyone from harm. That's God's job.
4. Those who know God's name trust in Him.

Lesson 5, Day Five

1. We don't need to fear failure or anything else, because no matter what, we have been redeemed by God; He knows us personally (calls us by name), and we belong to Him. When we are "passing through the waters" or "walking through fire" (both phrases that could describe what failure feels like), God does not abandon us. He remains with us, and keeps us safe. We may feel like we aren't going to make it, but God promises that we will not be swept away, burned, or consumed.
2. The precious blood of Christ purchased our redemption.
3. Our first step in decision-making is to ask God for wisdom. We need to have faith that God will guide us. An indecisive man is described as unstable. The unstable, unwise response after a time of prayer and discernment would be to continue to vacillate and procrastinate because of fear of failure or commitment.
4. God promises that He will bring something good from all our circumstances—even our mistakes. Even when there is no guarantee that our decision will bring us our desired result, we can be assured that God will teach or bless us in some way through it.

Prayer Pages

NOTES

walking with purpose

The Grail Prayer

Lord Jesus,
I give You my hands to do Your work.
I give You my feet to go Your way.
I give You my eyes to see as You do.
I give You my tongue to speak Your words.
I give You my mind that You may think in me.
I give You my spirit that You may pray in me.
Above all, I give You my heart that You may love in me
Your Father and all mankind.
I give You my whole self that You may grow in me,
So that it is You, Lord Jesus,
Who live and work and pray in me.

Prayer Requests

Date:

Date:

Prayer Requests

Date:

Date:

Prayer Requests

Date:

Date:

"For to the one who has, more will be given"
Matthew 13:12

CHRIST'S LOVE IS ENDLESS.

And the journey doesn't end here.

Walking With Purpose is more than a Bible study, it's a supportive community of women seeking lasting transformation of the heart. And you are invited.

Walking With Purpose believes that change happens in the hearts of women – and, by extension, in their families and beyond – through Bible study and community. We welcome all women, irrespective of faith background, age, or marital status.

Connect with us online for regular inspiration and to join the conversation. There you'll find insightful blog posts, Scriptures, and downloads.

For a daily dose of spiritual nourishment, join our community on Facebook, Twitter, Pinterest and Instagram.

And if you're so moved to start a Walking With Purpose study group at home or in your parish, take a look at our website for more information.

walkingwithpurpose.com

The Modern Woman's Guide to the Bible.

walking with purpose

NOTES

✲ DEEPEN YOUR FAITH ✲ OPEN YOUR ARMS ✲ BROADEN YOUR CIRCLE ✲

When your heart opens, and your love for Christ deepens, you may be moved to bring Walking With Purpose to your friends or parish. It's rewarding experience for many women who, in doing so, learn to rely on God's grace while serving Him.

If leading a group seems like a leap of faith, consider that you already have all the skills you need to share the Lord's Word:

- Personal commitment to Christ
- Desire to share the love of Christ
- Belief in the power of authentic, transparent community

The Walking With Purpose community supports you with:

- Training
- Mentoring
- Bible study materials
- Promotional materials

Few things stretch and grow our faith like stepping out of our comfort zone and asking God to work through us. Say YES, soon you'll see the mysterious and unpredictable ways He works through imperfect women devoted to Him.

Remember that if you humbly offer Him what you can, He promises to do the rest.

"See to it that no one misses the grace of God" Hebrews 12:15

Learn more about bringing Walking with Purpose to your parish.
Visit us at walkingwithpurpose.com
The Modern Woman's Guide To The Bible.

NOTES

NOTES

NOTES

NOTES

walking with purpose

Mission

Walking with Purpose transforms the hearts and lives of women by providing Bible studies that enable women to know Christ through Scripture and the teachings of the Roman Catholic Church.

Vision

To enable every Catholic woman in America to experience our life-changing Bible study, ***Opening Your Heart.***

Join us in transforming the hearts and lives of women.
Make a gift to Walking with Purpose today!

walkingwithpurpose.com/donate